The Economy of Brands

THE ECONOMY
OF BRANDS

Jan Lindemann

palgrave
macmillan

First published 2010 by
PALGRAVE MACMILLAN

Palgrave Macmillan in the UK is an imprint of Macmillan Publishers Limited,
registered in England, company number 785998, of Houndmills, Basingstoke,
Hampshire RG21 6XS.

Palgrave Macmillan in the US is a division of St Martin's Press LLC,
175 Fifth Avenue, New York, NY 10010.

Palgrave Macmillan is the global academic imprint of the above companies
and has companies and representatives throughout the world.

Palgrave® and Macmillan® are registered trademarks in the United States,
the United Kingdom, Europe and other countries.

ISBN 978–0–230–23250–1

This book is printed on paper suitable for recycling and made from fully
managed and sustained forest sources. Logging, pulping and manufacturing
processes are expected to conform to the environmental regulations
of the country of origin.

A catalogue record for this book is available from the British Library.

A catalog record for this book is available from the Library of Congress.

10   9   8   7   6   5   4   3   2   1
19 18 17 16 15 14 13 12 11 10

Printed and bound in Great Britain by
CPI Antony Rowe, Chippenham and Eastbourne

CONTENTS

LIST OF TABLES AND FIGURES

Tables

Figures

LIST OF ABBREVIATIONS

ABS	asset-backed security
BAV	brand asset valuator
B2B	business to business
B2C	business to consumer
BC	brand contribution
BC_L	brand contribution of the licensee
BE	brand earnings
BI	brand impact
BLR	brand license revenue
BR	brand royalty
CAPM	capital asset pricing model
CEO	chief executive officer
CFO	chief finance officer
CMO	chief marketing officer
CSR	corporate social responsibility
DCF	discounted cash flow
EBIT	earnings before interest and tax
EBITDA	earnings before interest, tax, depreciation, and amortization
EPS	earnings per share
FAS	Federal Accounting Standard
FRS	Financial Reporting Standard
GDP	gross domestic product
HR	human resources
IAS	International Accounting Standard
IE	intangible earnings
IFRS	International Financial Reporting Standard

IP	intellectual property
ISVC	International Standards Valuation Committee
KPI	key performance indicator
M&A	mergers and acquisitions
NPV	net present value
PPA	purchase price allocation
PR	public relations
R&D	research and development
ROE	return on equity
ROI	return on investment
SEM	structural equation modeling
SPV	special purpose vehicle
WACC	weighted average cost of capital

INTRODUCTION

The past 25 years have seen the recognition of intangible assets as the main drivers of business and shareholder value. In many businesses brands now account for the majority of shareholder value. This is not only true for the classic consumer goods businesses such as The Coca-Cola Company or Unilever but also for many B2B businesses selling to a professional audience. It is therefore important to understand how the economy of brands works and how it can be exploited to create sustainable value. The purpose of this book is to develop and enhance the understanding of the brand as an economic asset in order to make better business and investment decisions. It looks at the value creation of the brand from all aspects and provides approaches on how to assess and manage the value of brands. The book is written from a practitioners' perspective and is based on the author's experience in the practical application of brand value in all relevant areas.

Different chapters will consider the economic value of brands from a theoretical and practical point of view. The first chapter deals with the variety of definitions of brands and provides the economic definition of the brand adopted in this book. Chapter 2 looks at the relevance of brands as business assets and their contribution to business and shareholder value. The following chapters 3 to 7 discuss the emergence of the economic understanding of branding and layout in detail the main approaches to valuing brands including, in Chapter 7, a recommended brand valuation approach based on the author's experience and best industry practice. The eighth chapter examines the accounting debate on brands and intangible assets and its relevance for brand value. This is followed by a chapter describing how brands are used in large-scale debt securitizations in different types of financial transactions. Chapter 10 discusses the relevance of brand value in mergers and acquisitions (M&A) and how it can help in optimizing the outcomes. The licensing of brands to third parties as well as internally in the context of transfer pricing is discussed in Chapter 11. In the next chapter the brand value chain is developed and described as a framework for managing the brand's value creation. Chapter 13 discusses brand and marketing

1

ROI and provides an ROI framework that recognizes the long-term and accumulative value creation of brands. The stock market and investor perspective on brands and share price performance are investigated in Chapter 14. In the final chapter a brand management framework is discussed and developed. The findings and insights of the book are summed up in the Conclusion.

CHAPTER 1

WHAT IS A BRAND?

Understanding and measuring the economic value creation of brands requires a clear understanding and definition of what a brand is. The word brand is derived from the old Norse word "brenna" which means to burn. By burning signs onto cattle skin farmers could demonstrate their ownership. Although the initial purpose of branding was to demonstrate the origin of an animal it quickly grew into a means of differentiation. Over time a farmer would establish a certain reputation for the quality of his cattle expressed by the branded mark on the animal.[1] This enabled buyers to quickly assess the quality of the cattle and the price they were willing to pay for it. The information provided by the brand helped to guide the purchase decision. Facilitating choice is probably the most important purpose of branding in commerce. Understanding how the brand guides customer choice is crucial in defining what a brand is and what economic value it creates.

Brands can be traced back to ancient civilizations as evidenced by archeological proofs from Etruria, Greece, and Rome. Producers marked their pottery to communicate their origin and quality.[2] Branding became more widespread during the seventeenth and eighteenth centuries for porcelain, furniture, and tapestries. One of the oldest brands, the crossed swords of Meissen porcelain, stems from that period. However, it was the advent of mass produced packaged goods in the late-nineteenth century that made branding commercially important. Through industrialization the production of many household items, such as soap, moved from local production to centralized factories. As the distance between supplier and buyer widened the communication of origin and quality became more important. While mass-manufacturing provided economies of scale and often better product quality the goods needed to be sold to a wider market where customers were only familiar with local suppliers. The mass-manufacturers had to convince consumers, in the local markets, that their products were better than those of local producers. Packaging became the first means of differentiating their goods. It was during this period that brands such as Campbell's, Coca-Cola, and Quaker Oats emerged. In the US market these goods are still called "packaged goods."

In the late 1880s, James Walter Thompson, founder of the advertising company JWT and one of the pioneers of brand advertising, published so-called house advertisements to explain and sell the services of his agency to potential clients. Thompson drew on insights derived from behavioral psychology and advanced market research. His house advertisements were amongst the first systematic descriptions of the use and effect of brand advertising and an early commercial explanation of what is today defined as branding.[3] Consumer goods companies started developing sophisticated communications strategies including brand positioning, tag lines for advertising campaigns, packaging design, mascots, and jingles to build their brands through media communications mainly radio and television. By the 1940s, consumer marketing became more sophisticated as companies began to understand and recognize the social, psychological, and anthropological dimensions of the relationship consumers were developing with their brands. Increasingly brand communications expanded beyond promising quality towards building more complex psychological associations. As the quality of many products became increasingly similar and difficult to differentiate brands had to offer additional, mainly emotional benefits to be distinguishable. Most of these emotional benefits provide means of self-expression and definition. Buying and owning a specific brand communicates specific associations and values internally as well as externally. For example a buyer of a pair of Nike sport shoes communicates to both the outside world and the owner of the brand success, performance, and winning. Both internal and external communications are closely linked with the internal feeding on the external. Alongside the emotional benefits there are also perceptions about tangible or material brand benefits. In most categories consumers can choose from a wide range of options however, they can no longer test and compare the actual material differences of these offers. Some material benefits such as quality are also hard to define as they comprise different aspects such as durability, functionality, timeless design, etc. Often, therefore, consumers have to rely on the brand communications not only for intangible but also tangible benefits.

A brand is very complex object and according to current management theory and practice a brand can be defined in several ways. The narrower view defines the brand in terms of customers and consumers.

The wider view is more holistic and expands the brand across all business activities and beyond that to other entities and organizations such as people and countries. Traditional marketing definitions of brand have focused on its function of identifying and differentiating a company's products and services. The American Marketing Association defines a brand as "a name, term, design, symbol, or any other feature that identifies one seller's good or service as distinct from those of other sellers. The legal term for brand is trademark. A brand may identify one item, a family of items, or all items of that seller. If used for the firm as a whole, the preferred term is trade name."[4] Others have added the importance of the promise the brand makes to the potential buyer. In that context Philip Kottler, an American marketing guru, described a brand as a seller's promise to deliver a specific set of features, benefits, and services.[5] In a similar way, Walter Landor, founder of the equally named branding and design firm, defined the brand as "a promise. By identifying and authenticating a product or service it delivers a pact of satisfaction and quality."[6] Beyond the sheer promise, the experience of the brand is equally important. This leads to the more holistic view on branding according to which the brand is the result of all impressions and experiences the brand delivers. Ultimately, the brand is in the heads of the potential customers. David Aaker, marketing professor and creator of the term brand equity, sees the brand as "a set of assets (or liabilities) linked to the brand's name and symbol that adds to (or subtracts from) the value provided by a product or service."[7]

In financial terms, the brand constitutes an intangible asset that provides its owners with an identifiable and ownable cash flow over the time of its useful economic life. This can span more then 100 years as evidenced by brands such as Coca-Cola, Nokia, and Goldman Sachs. The brand is an economic asset that creates cash flows on a stand-alone basis (e.g. licensing) or integrated with other tangible and intangible assets. The cash flow impact is the main reason why businesses engage in building and maintaining their brand assets. The mental impact of branding is only economically relevant if it results in a positive financial return for the user or owner of the brand that outstrips the investments into the brand. The impact of brands on shareholder value is substantial and can amount up to 80 percent of shareholder value.

In its broadest definition, the brand can be defined as a conveyor of information. Contents and reception of this information define the scope and impact of the brand. As this book deals with the economic impact of brands it uses brand in the context of economically relevant transactions such as the sale and purchase of products and services. The information brands convey can be functional and emotional. Functional information ranges from factual elements such as origin, price, product features, and technical specifications to more general and less clearly defined elements such as functionality of product features, quality, consistency, and reliability. While the former can be tested and verified to some degree the latter are entirely subject to perception and judgment. Emotional information comprises, as the term suggests, all kind of emotions, feelings, moods, and attitudes. While functional information can in theory be factually verified emotional information is intangible and subjective. There are, however, many market research methods that can verify the emotional information. All brands have a combination of both elements although in very different proportions. Some brands focus mainly on the functional delivery others on emotional aspects. The functional aspects are important as in many cases they cannot be verified or tested by the audience to which they are communicated. Consumers buying a television will in most cases not be able to properly assess the technical quality of the product. Most flat panel TVs look very similar with little physical difference. Without a brand attached to them, choosing a television would be very difficult as consumers would be faced with a large number of flat boxes in black or silver. In addition to functional features, brands can communicate emotional aspects. Consumer electronics brands such as Sony and Samsung communicate prestige, status, and style in addition to their technical aspects. In cases of B2B and product-led brands, for example in technology, the functional information is always important and can at the extreme dominate the communication. In cases of famous iconic brands such as Coca-Cola, Marlboro and Nike the information is almost totally emotional with little or no functional contents.

The contents of the information can vary according to the audience the brand is addressing. Historically, brands were focused on consumers and customers in the context of the potential or actual purchase of goods and services. This is still the main task of brands and is at the core of brand management. However, with the recognition of the importance of corporate branding in the 1980s, the role of the brand has been extended to other internal and external audiences such as employees, suppliers, investors, regulators, and the general public thus blurring the differentiation between brand and corporate reputation.

While customers are still the main focus of branding activities worldwide the term brand has been expanded across a wide range of commercial activities and stakeholders. Countries, as well as individuals, can be brands. Most organizations have started embracing the concept of brand across stakeholders including customers, employees, investors, public institutions, public opinion, and suppliers. According to this wider interpretation of branding, the information it communicates facilitates a wide range of transactions: selling goods and services to consumers and customers; attracting and retaining employees; influencing capital markets; dealing with public institutions; and special interest groups.

There are several key components that constitute a brand. The most visible aspects are the trademarks and designs. They comprise brand names, logos, packaging designs, color schemes, shapes, and smells. These elements can be legally protected to provide their exclusive use. Most brands are based on a combination of several trademarks. In the case of Coca-Cola these are the Coca-Cola name, the signature style of the name, the dynamic ribbon under the name, the waisted bottle shape, the combination of colors, and many of the company's slogans, the most famous being "It's the real thing." Increasingly, companies have extended their trademark protection to jingles, smells, and shapes. In 1994, Harley-Davidson Inc. filed the engine "roar" exhaust sound of its v-twin motorcycle engines as a trademark but withdrew it a couple of years later due to strong opposition from competitors which made a successful application highly unlikely. Nevertheless, the Harley example demonstrates how complex and sophisticated the legal protection of brands has become. The exclusive ownership and control of the overall mix of the different brand elements is crucial as it allows their owners to identify and distinguish their products and services. Identification and differentiation are the most basic commercial functions of brands. They establish a clear link between a product or service and its provider. Once the origin of a product and service can be identified other functions follow.

Patents for technologies and formulas can also form part of the brand. Most pharmaceutical brands are linked to patents. The secret formula for the Coca-Cola syrup is also a core brand element. The Microsoft brand is linked to several patents and technologies.

Due to the importance of the legal protection of their brands to their business, brand-owning companies fiercely protect their trademarks around the world. Most companies have trademark experts in their legal department and employ IP lawyers to protect their brands and initiate legal actions against the slightest possible infringement.

Lindt & Sprüngli, the Swiss chocolate makers, have for many years been entrenched in a legal battle to prevent a German chocolate manufacturer from selling gold-wrapped chocolate bunnies in order to protect their famous golden chocolate bunnies.[8] The World Customs Organization estimates that counterfeit goods account for between 5 to 7 percent of global merchandise trade, amounting to US$450 billion.[9] China alone is estimated to be contributing to almost two-thirds of all the fake and pirated goods worldwide. LVMH, the French luxury group, spends more than US$16 million annually on legal investigations and procedures against counterfeiting.[10]

All these legal rights are important as they represent the "tangible" and most visible elements of the brand that trigger its specific associations and values that materialize in cash flows generated from customers' purchases of the brand.

A meaningful concept of brand which is adopted throughout this book defines the brands as an intangible asset that creates and secures identifiable cash flows by combining symbols, associations, and perception in a unique manner that motivate consumers to choose and purchase a company's goods and services in preference to its competitors. The associations and perceptions are the result of a company's actions and communications as an entity. The brand evolves out of the expectations it generates and experiences it delivers. Both factors are closely intertwined. Brand communications and experiences can be systematically managed to maximize a company's cash flow generation.

CHAPTER 2

THE VALUE OF BRANDS

The value of brands materializes in several ways. The most direct and obvious is the sale of products and services to consumers. The combination of the price paid for a product plus the quantity and frequency of purchase creates the sales revenues for a business. This is converted into profits and ultimately shareholder value. The share price of a company is driven by investor's expectations about the future ability of the business to attract customer revenue and extract profits from these. The value of brands also materializes in mergers and acquisitions, the subsequent balance sheet recognition, licensing, and other financial transactions such as securitizations.

BRANDS AS INTANGIBLE ASSETS

Intangible assets have become the key driver of shareholder value. Over the past 25 years the average price-to-tangible book value of the S&P 500 (a value-weighted index published since 1957 of the prices of 500 large-cap common stocks actively traded in the United States) has been about 3.9 meaning that investors valued the companies included in the S&P 500 close to four times their tangible net assets (see Figure 2.1). In this context it is important to note that the S&P 500 index includes a wide range of B2B businesses as well as companies from the energy, resources, and manufacturing industries that have traditionally been more physical asset heavy. The time period also includes several business cycles and stock market bull and bear phases. The average price to tangible book value of the S&P 500 rose steadily from an average of around 1.4 at the beginning of the 1980s to around 3.1 in the mid-1990s. It accelerated rapidly in the late 1990s to exceed 7.0 during the dotcom bubble before falling back to 2.7 during the 2008/9 stock market crash. The long-term price to tangible book value of 3.9 indicates that the tangible assets of a business (land, equipment, inventory, net working capital,

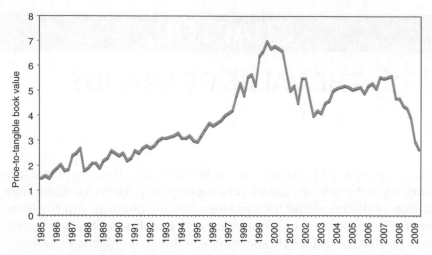

FIGURE 2.1 **S&P 500 price to tangible book value**
Source: Bloomberg, 2009.

etc.) account for about a quarter of the value that investors are placing on a company. The remaining three-quarters are accounted for by intangible assets such as patents, business systems, distribution rights, brands, customer databases, and the quality of a company's management and workforce. Although book and market value are only partially comparable, as most accounting items are cost based and the share price represents investors' expectations of the future cash flows of a business, the price to tangible book value provides a sufficiently clear indication that investors see the majority of value in a company's intangible assets.

Among all intangible assets the brand is unique with respect to its durability and holistic nature. Brands can maintain their leading position over long periods of time. Some of the worlds leading brands such as Coca-Cola, Gillette, and Goldman Sachs are over 100 years old. Most brands outlive all other business assets. Brands are also more holistic than other assets as they are the combined result of all customer experiences and communications. Ultimately, brands represent the relationship between a company and its customers who generate its revenues through buying its products and services. This is supported by the fact that consumer and brand related spending accounted in 2008 for 72 percent of US gross domestic product.[1] That means that nearly two-thirds of the GDP of the world's largest economy are tied to brands and their value generation.

EMERGING RECOGNITION OF THE VALUE OF BRANDS

Although brands have been important business assets since the early days of commerce and larger scale manufacturing, the wider recognition of their role in business is the result of the M&A activity of the late-1980s and early-1990s when a number of companies with strong brands were taken over. In 1988, Nestlé bought Rowntree for UK£2.8 billion or five times its book value and in the same year Philip Morris bought Kraft General Foods for US$12.9 billion at a multiple of six times its book value. About 90 percent of the value was represented by the Kraft Food's brand portfolio.[2] These large takeover multiples demonstrated the importance of the value of brands and intangible assets relative to the value of the tangible assets such as land and manufacturing facilities. This led to a growing interest in brands and other intangible assets from both the accountancy profession and the executive suite. The accounting profession was primarily interested in updating the treatment of what had, up until then, been termed "goodwill" (defined as the difference between the purchase price of a company and the book value of its assets). As long as this difference was relatively modest, goodwill was regarded as a minor balancing item rather than a serious valuation issue. As the portion of goodwill in transactions increased, and often dwarfed the value of tangible assets, it became necessary to be more specific about its definition and accounting treatment. The United Kingdom was the first market to react by introducing in 1998 the Financial Reporting Standard 10. In 2001, the United States followed suit with the Financial Accounting Standard 141 and in 2005, the International Financial Reporting Standard 3 was published laying out the internationally agreed way of accounting for goodwill in acquisitions. Since then many companies such as The Coca-Cola Company, Vodafone, AT&T, P&G, LVMH, Prada, L'Oréal, have included the value of their acquired brands on the balance sheet.

There is a wide range of intangible assets. Patents are intangible assets and so is human capital. Accounting standards have tried to bundle them into different classes to ease their assessment and valuation. According to international accounting standards there are marketing related, customer related, artistic, contractual, and technology related intangible assets. Brands according to the definition developed in Chapter 1 fall mainly into the first two categories. However, the complexity of branding according to current management thinking does not fit the accounting approach. In order to understand and quantify how much brands contribute to shareholder value one needs to step beyond the accounting definition and look at the meaning and effect brands have on a business. If the brand is the key driver of customer or consumer choice then its importance relative to the other intangible assets must be significant.

THE ROLE OF BRANDS IN BUSINESS

The most acclaimed management gurus have acknowledged the important role of branding and marketing. Peter Drucker, the management guru credited with the creation of management science, famously stated that "business has only two functions – marketing and innovation."[3] Later, Michael Porter, another management guru who conceptualized competitive advantage, argued that competitive advantage is a function of either providing comparable buyer value more efficiently than competitors (lower cost), or performing activities at comparable cost but in unique ways that create more buyer value than competitors and, hence, command a premium price, i.e. differentiation through branding. According to Porter, you win either by being cheaper or by being different, that is, being perceived by the customer as better or more relevant.[4] These examples give some indication about the unique nature of brands over and above other assets. With global competition and excess capacity in virtually every industry, brands are crucial for communicating why a company's products and services are uniquely able to satisfy customer needs. In an environment where the functional differences between products and services have nearly vanished, brands provide the basis for establishing meaningful differences between competing offers.

In most categories the choice of offers is overwhelming. From television to mobile phones, telecommunication networks, watches, electricity tariffs, cars, detergents, cornflakes, mustard, chocolate, life insurance, investment funds, shampoo, fashion, etc. there is a plethora of offers to chose from. In the majority of these categories quality is more a perception than a reality. The automotive market is a good example in this respect. The massive improvements in inherent automobile quality over the past decade mean that reliability and functionality are no longer a basis for differentiation. Today, most cars on offer are well built. According to a J.D. Power survey, (a US based marketing services information firm best known for its customer satisfaction research on new-car quality and long-term dependability) the overall quality of cars between 1998 and 2008 improved from an average of 1.76 problems per vehicle to 1.18 problems per vehicle. Comparing the best and worst performers demonstrates the insignificance of the difference in performance between different car brands. According to the 2008 survey, Jeep had 1.67 problems per vehicle while Porsche had 0.87 problems per vehicle. Problems here include every minor failure such as car seat heating and other gadgets.[5] While the actual quality difference is negligible it offers marketing opportunities for the brands topping the list. Lexus is a brand that has marketed itself heavily on its performance in the J.D Power surveys. However, this is more about perception of quality than actual difference. Perceived quality is only one of many factors that drive customer choice in cars. The purchase is driven by a complex mix of design, price, incentives, dealer networks, features, drive experience, and fuel economy among others. In any given car category there are sufficient choices on offer that do not differ by quality or other technical features. They do, however, differ by the way they are perceived by potential buyers and it is their perception that determines the purchase.

There are many other examples that demonstrate how businesses depend heavily on the intangible asset brand. Water is a great example for the economic impact of branding. Water is in most developed economies a commodity paid for through utility bills. However, branded bottled water has become a major market over the past 10 years exceeding US$50 billion in 2008.[6] Bottled water is offered at very different price points. For example, consumers in the UK are willing to pay 141 times more for a liter of Evian water than for tap water. This is even more surprising when blind tests revealed that more than half of participants could not taste a difference between the tap and the bottled water and some even preferred the taste of tap water.[7] Consumers are willing to pay this enormous price premium because they perceive bottled water to be purer, cleaner, and ultimately healthier. This perception continues despite the fact that in most OECD countries health regulations regarding tap water are more stringent and strict than is the case for bottled water. Water in plastic bottles is often treated with radiation to kill potential germs and allow its storage for many years. In addition, there are many brands such as Aquafina and Dasani that sell reprocessed municipal water which is basically tap water. Clearly, consumers are not paying a high premium for the functional benefit of drinking water but the brand promise of a pure and healthy lifestyle. Similar dynamics can be found in other categories. There are luxury watches with complicated automatic movements and precious metals selling for thousands of dollars that are less accurate than watches with a quartz movement selling for less than US$50. A Cartier lady's watch with a quartz movement in stainless steel costs around US$2,000 – a similar watch made from the same materials also with a quartz movement can be bought for a fraction of the price.

In 2008, Smart, a brand of Daimler AG's personal car group, introduced a 10 year anniversary model designed by Hermès International, a leading French fashion group. While the Smart usually retails for around US$14,000, the special Hermès edition costs about US$48,000, over three times that of the standard model.[8] The premium is not paid for the fine leather interior or coloring but for the co-branding with Hermès.

The impact of branding is not limited to the B2C market. The professional buyer is equally prone to the influence of brand perceptions when choosing a supplier or firm. From financial services to IT systems the choice is from a wide range of similar offers.[9] For example, a survey by UBS in 2003 found that there was very little differentiation between banks on the key attributes on which customers choose their investment bank.[10] Most of them can produce similar expertise, experience, and track records. Nevertheless, fear, uncertainty, and doubt also known as FUD lead many professional buyers to seek the services of established brands. There is also the glamor and perception of success that drive many senior executives to buy the services of famous consulting and advisory firms. These brands are also often used to enable and support change and senior executive decisions. After all, if firms such as McKinsey or Goldman Sachs suggest certain strategies and transactions it is implied that as the best of their breed they will be the right decisions. This is epitomized by the traditional axiom of purchasing agents that "nobody ever got fired for buying IBM equipment."[11] It is therefore not surprising to find among the top leading global brands B2B brands such as IBM, Intel, Microsoft, and GE.

BRANDS AND SHAREHOLDER VALUE

The specific value that brands contribute to shareholder value has been most prominently demonstrated by the "Best Global Brands" survey published in *BusinessWeek* in cooperation with Interbrand annually since 2001. This ranking has been most influential in boardrooms and among c-level executives around the world. Based on a survey of

TABLE 2.1 **Selected brand values according to brand value surveys published in 2009**

Brand value in $ million	BusinessWeek/ Interbrand	Millward Brown	Brand Finance	Brand value average	% of market capital
Coca-Cola	68,734	67,625	32,728	56,362	49
IBM	60,211	66,662	31,530	52,801	34
GE	47,777	59,793	26,654	44,741	30
Nokia	34,864	35,163	19,889	29,972	74
Apple	15,433	63,113	13,648	30,731	21
McDonald's	32,275	66,575	20,003	39,618	65
HSBC	10,510	19,079	25,364	18,318	17
American Express	14,971	14,963	9,944	13,293	37
Google	31,980	100,039	29,261	53,760	38
Nike	13,179	11,999	14,583	13,254	48

Sources: Compiled from Best Global Brand 2008; BrandZ Top 100, 2009; Global 500, 2009.

leading global companies, this ranking has continuously been voted by leading PR-firm Burson-Marsteller among the top most influential reputation rankings.[12] The survey has firmly established the importance of branding among CEOs and other senior management worldwide. The author of this book established and has managed this survey for a considerable time. Many companies have utilized the survey for benchmarking or as KPI for their marketing executives. According to the *BusinessWeek* survey, brands account on average for more than one-third of shareholder value. Other firms have also published brand values most notably market research firm Millward Brown and brand valuation specialist BrandFinance although these surveys do not have a comparable reputation to the *BusinessWeek* study. Despite significant valuation differences between these surveys, they all demonstrate the substantial value brands contribute to shareholder value. For example, the value of the McDonalds brand accounts, according to the average brand value of all three surveys, for 65 percent of the company's stock market value (see Table 2.1).

The rankings clearly show that brands do not only contribute significant value to consumer focused business but also B2B businesses such as IBM and GE. In the case of IBM, for example, the brand accounts for 34 percent of shareholder value. For most companies the brand represents the largest business asset.

Several studies have used the brand values published in the Best Global Brands survey to prove the shareholder value impact of brands.

These studies compared the performance of companies with strong brands featured in the survey with a market portfolio representing the rest of the stock market in the US. According to their findings a portfolio based on brand value significantly outperforms the market portfolio with respect to both return and risk. The brand portfolio showed a monthly return of 64 basis points (0.64 percent) or 48 percent above the market portfolio excluding the companies in the brand portfolio. At the same time the brand value weighted portfolio had a significantly lower risk profile than the market. Its beta, a financial measure for risk, was 0.85 or 15 percent lower than the market portfolio.[13] This research demonstrates that strong brands can provide a business with sustainable higher returns than the market at significantly lower risk. Other published studies based on brand values show a similar outperformance of stocks with strong brands relative to key indices such as the S&P 500 and the MSCI World Index, a stock market index consisting of 1,500 stocks of companies from 29 countries.[14]

The success of the Best Global Brands has led many other institutions to publish brand value rankings on a local and global scale. As most of these cover a much shorter time period they have not been academically verified in the same way as the Best Global Brands survey. Institutions that provide brand value rankings include Millward Brown, Brand Finance, and Intangible Business. Although all these surveys identify a significant value variance for the same brands they confirm the overall value creation of brands[15]

Several rationales support the hypothesis that brand value is linked to the market value of a firm's equity. For example, high brand value smoothes earnings in cyclical industries or in general periods of lower sales. During these downturns, consumers tend to spend less. As consumers are comfortable with highly regarded brands, sales of these products tend not to decline as much as the industry in general. Brand value also provides protection from competitors due to increased customer loyalty. Overall, companies with stronger brands do not suffer as much from external threats and, therefore, are less likely to experience financial distress.

THE VALUE OF BRANDS IN MERGERS AND ACQUISITIONS

The value of brands is also evidenced by their increasing importance in large financial transactions. One of the largest leveraged buyouts was completed on the back of a strong portfolio of brands. In 1988, KKR one of the pioneers of leveraged buyouts acquired RJR Nabisco for US$31.4 billion. The portfolio included iconic brands such as Oreo, Ritz, Camel, and Winston. Two recent transactions in the spirits industry illustrate the value an even relatively recently created brand can achieve. In August 2005 Bacardi acquired Grey Goose Vodka for US$2.2 billion, 15 times its EBITDA (earnings before interest, tax depreciation and amortization) or 4.7 times its annual revenue. The brand was created in 1998 and became the leading premium vodka brand in the US by 2003. In 2008, 3 years later, Pernod Ricard acquired Vin & Sprit for €5.6 billion implying a EBITDA multiple of 20.8.[16] The main asset of this transaction was the Absolut brand which was created in 1979. The acquisition multiple topped even the heady price Bacardi had paid for Grey Goose Vodka. In 2005 SBC Communications one of the leading regional telecoms in the US acquired AT&T for US$16 billion. Although the AT&T brand had a 120 year history its reputation had suffered in the recent past. The announcement of SBC's CEO Edward E. Whitacre Jr. that the new company would adopt the AT&T brand came to the surprise of many marketing experts. Whitacre quoted the brand's heritage and its international recognition as the main reasons for adopting the AT&T brand for the merged businesses. The value of the AT&T brand in the acquisition price of US$16 billion amounted to US$4.9 billion, or 31 percent of the company's value.[17]

The high multiples that have been paid for businesses with strong brands match the findings of the stock market performance of companies with strong brands. In most businesses brands are a key value driver and often the single most valuable business asset. However, their value is not static and requires careful handling and management. In order to assess the economic value of brands it is therefore crucial to have a clear understanding of how this value is generated. The following chapters will explore methods and techniques for valuing brands and how to use them to optimize the value creation of brands.

CHAPTER 3

ASSESSING THE VALUE OF BRANDS

INTRODUCTION

Since brands have become such important business assets there is a need for management to understand and assess their economic value creation. There are three main reasons why management has become interested in the value of brands. The first is to manage and improve the performance of the company selling the branded products and services promoting customer desires to purchase in greater quantities and more frequently. Second, management must know the value of its brands when it is involved in a range of financial transactions including licensing, tax planning, M&A, franchising, financing, and investor communications. Third, the accounting requirements for acquired goodwill and intangible assets, which include brands, need to be met. Most accounting standards require a financial value for an acquired brand in order to capitalize it as an intangible asset on the balance sheet and subject it to annual impairment tests. These demonstrate the need for the financial valuation of the brand so that it can be properly managed and used in financial transactions.

Traditionally, brand assessment was the realm of the marketing department and focused on researching perception and behaviors of actual and potential consumers. Qualitative and quantitative research studies are conducted to understand whether or not consumers were aware of the brand (awareness), what they knew about the brand (knowledge), their perception of the brand, whether they would consider purchasing the brand, whether they have purchased the brand, whether they intend to buy the brand in the future or will continue buying the brand (loyalty). There is no doubt that these marketing indicators provide valuable information that is crucial for managing brands. However, they are not sufficient for an economic assessment of a brand – a clear link to financial outcomes is required. Ultimately, marketing indicators are only relevant as long as they can demonstrate their financial value. Whether it be market share, a certain image factor, consideration or customer satisfaction they are only worth analyzing and tracking if they produce financial results. In most companies senior management is rewarded according to financial performance targets and investors base their assessment of a company's performance on its financial results such as revenue growth, EBITDA, cash flow, and return on equity. With the increased awareness and acceptance of intangibles such as brands as key drivers of shareholder value the need to understand and measure the financial value of brands has emerged.

HISTORY OF BRAND VALUATION

Brand valuation emerged out of the takeover boom of the 1980s when highly leveraged dealmakers pursued undervalued assets. An example was the Hanson Trust, a UK takeover vehicle, which in 1986 acquired the Imperial Group for UK£2.3 billion. Although the main business of Imperial was tobacco the company also owned a significant food business. Shortly after the acquisition Hanson sold off the food business for UK£2.1 billion retaining the highly cash generating tobacco business for which it had only paid a net price of just UK£200 million. This transaction showed that accountants as well as stock analysts were substantially undervaluing brand assets. In 1988, two years after the Hanson deal, another UK food group became the target of a highly leveraged bid. The target company was Rank Hovis McDougall (RHM) a food business with a strong local brand portfolio including Bisto, Hovis, and Saxa. The raider was the Australian takeover specialist Goodman Fielder Wattie (GFW). GFW approached investors with a bid price for RHM's shares that valued the company at a small premium over its net assets. RHM's management felt that the bid substantially undervalued the business as it did not take into account its portfolio of valuable brands. In order to prove its point, management decided to undertake a financial valuation of its brand portfolio in order to record it as an intangible asset on its balance sheet. At the time this was a rather radical idea. RHM contacted a small brand consulting firm called Interbrand to assist. Interbrand approached the London Business School for support and together they developed the first documented model for valuing brands as assets in their own rights. The approach combined financial and marketing analyses.

The valuation method was a "multiples" approach where earnings attributed to a brand were multiplied with a factor determined by the strength of the brand. The overall result was a financial value for each brand within RHM's portfolio. The brand portfolio was valued at UK£678 million while the tangible assets on the balance sheet had been valued at less then UK£400 million. The value of the brand portfolio was recognized on the balance sheet increasing the total assets to more than UK£1.2 billion. Putting the value of the brands on the balance sheet resulted in investors re-valuing RHM's business. The company share price increased significantly and GFW withdrew its offer. Through this action RHM was the first publicly–listed company to record its internally generated brand portfolio as intangible assets on the balance sheet.

Later, the diversified food Group Grand Metropolitan put its acquired brands on its balance sheet. RHM's actions sparked a lengthy debate among all key constituencies such as companies as well as accounting and government bodies about the value of brands and intangible assets. Ultimately, this debate resulted in changing the balance sheet treatment of intangibles in accounting standards around the world. More importantly, the finance function within businesses became interested in the use of brand valuation for practical purposes, transforming it into a common language for finance and marketing.

Over the two decades following the valuation of RHM's brand portfolio, many approaches and methodologies for valuing brands emerged. Although there is an on-going debate within the financial and marketing community about the appropriate valuation methods and purposes, some common views and directions have emerged.[1]

At the same time as companies in the UK started using brand valuation to prop up their balance sheets, which triggered the debate on the accounting treatment of intangible assets, the marketing community also started to define brand as an intangible asset under the label of "brand equity." Although equity is a financial term, marketers used it to define a set of market research based metrics indicating that brands are valuable long-term business assets. The term gained widespread acceptance throughout the marketing community mainly through the writings of David Aaker[2] and Kevin Lane Keller.[3] Although brand equity was never defined in financial terms, it was assumed that brand equity would create economic value.

20

The aim of brand equity was to go beyond a hotchpotch of market research metrics and develop a comprehensive framework that linked brand perception with customers' purchase intentions and loyalty. Many of the leading market research firms, such as Research International's Equity Engine, Young & Rubicam's BrandAsset Valuator, Ipsos's Equity Builder, and Millward Brown's BrandDynamics which became later BrandZ, developed their own version of measuring brand equity. Each version involves understanding the sources of brand equity (typically functional equity, emotional equity, and price) and measuring the strength of customer engagement with the brand. The main drawback of these approaches remained the fact that a financial impact of brand equity was always implied but was never explicit. As such these methods remained in the realm of marketing and did not penetrate the mindset of the financial community or the board room.

However, when marketing and financial analyses were combined it became possible to identify and quantify the economic value of brands. Then brand valuation achieved success in the c-suite. CEOs and CFOs of the leading global companies have consistently voted the brand value survey published annually in *BusinessWeek* as among the top 4 business rankings. There are many approaches and models for assessing the value of brands. Most marketing agencies offer their own version of brand equity or brand valuation as a "proprietary" approach. However, all relevant approaches fall broadly into three categories.

The first category comprises of market-research-based models that measure different dimensions of a brand to assess the relationship consumers have with the brand. These models are categorized under the term *brand equity*. Despite the use of the financial term, equity, these models are neither designed nor equipped to provide a financial value for the brand. Instead they attempt to measure the strength of the relationship consumers have with the brand. The strength is measured according to a range of dimensions deemed to be relevant in determining this relationship. The measured brand dimensions are either reported separately or linked through statistical analyses that measure the relative strength of this relationship. The more sophisticated approaches focus on consumers' consideration and purchase intent. Although the thinking and principles behind these models provide valuable insights they do not deliver an economic assessment of the brand. Most of these models were developed to assess the effectiveness of marketing communications not the financial value of the brand.

The second category of valuation approaches consist of purely financial approaches that are designed to provide a financial value for a brand. These methods are rooted in traditional corporate finance theory and value a brand according to the same principles as businesses and other commercial assets. Several methods fall into this category. The main ones are income-based and comparables approaches. They are used mainly for assessing brand values for commercial transactions and financial reporting. Beyond the financial figure obtained they provide little or no insight on the relationship between consumer perceptions and intentions and financial value generation. The predominantly financial analysis is assumed to include all relevant information required to assess the economic value generation of a brand.

The third category blends financial and marketing approaches to understand and assess the economic value of brands. These approaches derive a financial sum based on consumer insights and financial analysis. Only a few approaches systematically integrate marketing and financial analyses. The majority is based on brand equity models with an "add on" financial module. The blended approaches use behavioral and perceptive research data to inform financial forecasting (in particular revenue generation) and are among the most sophisticated and complex approaches.

The following chapters will provide further details and a discussion of the different categories concluding with a recommended framework.

CHAPTER 4

BRAND EQUITY: THE MARKETER'S VIEW ON BRAND VALUE

At the time financial markets started recognizing the value of intangible assets and brands marketing academics in the US, in the early-1990s, also attempted to conceptualize the brand as a business asset. The result was the concept of brand equity which capitalized on a financial term to define a marketing concept. The term was made popular by the publications of David Aaker and Kevin Keller. Aaker described brand equity as a "set of assets (and liabilities) linked to a brand's name and symbol that adds to (or subtracts from) the value provided by a product or service to a firm and /or that firm's customers."[1] The main asset categories comprised awareness, loyalty, perceived quality, and other brand specific associations. Despite the use of the term equity, the framework consisted of a combination of market research metrics. Aaker later expanded the framework to include metrics from other models, most notably Y&R's brand asset evaluator and Interbrand's brand strength assessment. The resulting measurement framework comprised the following metrics:

1. willingness to pay a price premium;
2. satisfaction/loyalty;
3. perceived quality;
4. leadership/popularity;
5. esteem/respect;
6. perceived value;
7. personality;
8. trust and admiration for the organization;
9. differentiation;
10. market share;
11. price differential; and
12. distribution depth/coverage.

As the broad set of metrics suggests the framework is more a guidance for the issues and themes to consider than a clear quantitative model. Aaker acknowledged that while all these measures have diagnostic value, management efforts should focus on a minimum of one to a maximum of four relevant metrics. Selecting the relevant metrics requires educated judgment. As the weighting of the factors can be a conceptual as well as statistical challenge in its own right, Aaker suggested that weighting all dimensions equally would be a good default option.[2] As a single measure for brand equity Aaker favors the price premium as the most suitable metric.

Aaker's brand equity framework is useful as it provides a list of proven and relevant metrics. It also clearly demonstrates the complexity of and difficulty involved in measuring the economic value of brands. However, the model does not address two key elements that are crucial for valuing and managing the economic value of brands. The first element is the relative importance or prioritization of different dimensions. The different dimensions overlap and it is not clear how dependent or independent each dimension is. An understanding of the relative impact and weight of each element is critical for recognizing and managing the value creation of a brand. Second, the framework lacks a clear conceptual link to financial value creation. An economic assessment of a brand is incomplete without a link to financially measurable business results. As such, Aaker's brand equity framework provides useful insights and concepts for assessing brand value, but on its own it cannot provide an economic assessment of a brand.

After Aaker, Kevin Keller, a marketing professor from the Tuck School of Business at Dartmouth, developed a systematic brand equity approach in the form of a pyramid shaped model that has influenced several research models. He also collaborated with some research agencies, most notably with the Nielsen Company, on commercially applied brand equity models which are described later. At the base of the pyramid is the salience of the brand. On the next level, the brand is split into its rational and emotional aspects measured in terms of performance and imagery. Consumer judgments and feelings about the brand occupy the layer above. At the tip of the pyramid is brand resonance measured by loyalty, attachment, community, and engagement. The customers' relationship with a brand can be measured in terms of their position on the pyramid of engagement and their relative bias towards a rationally dominant or emotionally dominant relationship.[3]

While Aaker formulated the brand equity manifesto several market research companies have developed models that deliver an integrated brand equity approach based on the relative impact of different brand dimensions. One of the most prominent and longest running approaches has been the brand asset valuator (BAV) developed in 1993 by Young & Rubicam, a major advertising firm.[4] The BAV is a brand equity model based on a standardized questionnaire that is used to assess thousands of brands in major markets around the world. As such it is among the largest and most consistent market research survey available. The assessment model is based on a 32-item questionnaire that is analyzed according to four major brand dimensions: differentiation; relevance; esteem; and knowledge. Differentiation measures how distinctive and differentiated a brand is. The more differentiated a brand is, the more it stands out and represents a point of view. Relevance measures how meaningful and important the brand is relative to the respondents' needs. Esteem measures popularity and perceived quality of the brand. Knowledge measures the understanding respondents have of what the brand stands for. The BAV measures the health of a brand by mapping the research results on a two-dimensional matrix called the "power grid."

The X-axis measures brand stature which is calculated by multiplying esteem with knowledge. The Y-axis measures brand strength which is calculated by multiplying differentiation with relevance. The equity of a brand can be assessed according to its position on this power grid. As with most 2×2 matrices the best performers can be found in the quadrant on the upper right. Here lie the healthy and leading brands that score highly on both dimensions. According to the 2006 survey, brands from the consumer electronics category included Sony, LG, I-Pod, Duracell, and Energizer. The bottom left quadrant is made up of newcomers or weak brands that have failed to develop. Here we find Blaupunkt, Loewe, and Technics. In the top left quadrant are the growing or strong niche brands such as Miele, Dyson, and Bang & Olufsen. In the right bottom quadrant is populated by established but tired and declining brands such as Whirlpool, GE, and Toshiba.[5]

The brand asset valuator is a unique market research study that provides interesting benchmarks and insights. However, it does not link directly to economic value creation. This may be due to the fact that it was established by Y&R with the intention of assessing communications effectiveness through consumer perceptions. Due to its adoption as an operating unit within Y&R Group, the BAV has been positioned as a marketing consultation product. In that context there have been several attempts to overlay the BAV database with some financial analyses. In 2002, Y&R formed a joint venture with Stern Stewart & Co named BrandEconomics. The venture undertook a study comparing the intangible value of companies where one brand dominated the business (more than 80 percent of revenues) and which were quoted on the stock market with the results from the BAV brand health check. The intangible value was calculated as the stock market value less the tangible book value. BrandEconomics then derived sales multiples by dividing the branded sales with the intangible value. These multiples were compared with the results of the BAV matrix. It should be noted that the study covered the period between 1993 and 2000 when the price to tangible book value of the S&P 500 Index was between 3 and 7. This period was one of the biggest bull markets and it ended with the dotcom bubble burst in March 2000. As a result BrandEconomics' analysis is based on a rather unrepresentative set of data that limits the use of the analysis and in particular its generalization and application to other periods.

The study demonstrated that there was a match between the relative health of a brand as measured by the BAV and its value creation. Companies with relatively unknown brands had a relatively low intangible value equal to around 0.9 of their annual revenues. Stronger brands with higher levels of differentiation and relevance had approximately double the intangible value at 1.9 times their annual sales. Brands that have both strength and stature were unsurprisingly the healthiest brands. The intangible value of these companies reached 2.5 times their annual sales. However, companies with high strength but low differentiation showed a significantly lower intangible value of 1.4 times their annual revenues. These companies were "milking" their brands but failed to deliver a relevant and differentiated offer which is reflected in declining price points. BrandEconomics' research also concluded that, on average, financial factors explained around 55 percent of the market value of companies, brand factors around 25 percent and other factors such as industry context and economic cycle accounting for most of the remaining 20 percent.

However, the brand impact on stock market value showed a rather broad range between 10 percent and 75 percent suggesting a higher brand influence in consumer goods than B2B and technology driven companies. The research also showed that there was a strong link between differentiation and higher profit margins. Differentiation did not only match higher profit margins but also stronger protection during the recession period of 1999 to 2001. Brands with strong differentiation managed largely to preserve their levels of operating profit.[6]

The BrandEconomics research revealed that relevance and differentiation are the key drivers of brand and shareholder value. As such it provided further quantitative support for an established marketing mantra. The impact depended on the relative importance of branding in the respective business. The venture between Y&R and Stern Stewart was short-lived and dissolved a year later. Due to the lack of integration between marketing and financial analysis the findings were too broad to assist in brand strategy and detailed brand building efforts. An additional issue was that the intangible valuations were performed during a strong bull market run resulting in high price to tangible book value. This limits the application of the specific figures to other periods where the price to book ratios were significantly lower. In 2009 the price to tangible book value of the S&P 500 dropped to 2.7. Interestingly, the BAV team used the stock market decline to put an alternative spin on their database. The bull run that provided the data to support the link between the findings of the BAV research and financial impact was now used to identify a "brand bubble," a theme that was turned into a book and an accompanying website.[7] Now the BAV team claimed that there was a bubble in the S&P 500 market capitalization of the magnitude of US$4 trillion twice the size of the subprime mortgage market accounting for about a third of all shareholder value.

An analysis of 15 years of research data from the BAV survey suggested that relevance and in particular differentiation of the majority of brands had severely deteriorated. The authors claimed that investors had a dramatically inflated view of the value of brands. It assumed that analysts and investors were actually aware of the value of brands and that they were pricing these into their valuations of quoted companies. It may well be that many brands received lower scores in the BAV survey. However, that does not necessarily match with the stock market performance. GE and Starbucks are among the top performers in the BAV matrix but investors have obviously ignored these insights as these stocks lost significant value in the 2008 recession. Zara, on the other hand, performs poorly although the share price of its holding company Inditex Group lost significantly less in the same period. It is not that Starbucks and GE are not strong brands. In fact, they are very valuable brands with GE being among the top ten most valuable brands in published brand surveys. What is uneasy about the BAV analysis is the fact that for many prominent brands the BAV results do not match financial performance and stock market valuations. The overall assumption that stock markets were overvaluing brands for a decade is hard to believe and prove. There is little evidence that analysts and investors are strongly focusing on brand health or value in making investment recommendations or decisions. Although there are examples where analysts will comment on the brands of a specific business they are considering they will be marginal relative to the financial assessment. It is the biggest complaint of most marketers and CMOs that analysts do not pay sufficient, if any, attention to branding and marketing. This is less surprising if one understands on what analytical basis shares are traded. Analysts look at past and in particular expected financial performance of businesses, market dynamics, and valuations as well as macroeconomic trends. The hard core quantitative funds have built sophisticated computer models analyzing nearly all data available to identify predictable patterns for their investment strategies. In this context brand specific data are rare and minor in influence.[8] What is mainly impacting stock prices is the financial effect of branding and marketing such as higher revenues, profits, and cash flows. The assumption of BAV's brand bubble hypothesis is undermined by several key facts. First, brand perceptions are currently peripheral to most analysts' and investors' sentiments. It is therefore hard to argue that the changes in the BAV surveys have a significant impact on share prices. There also appears to be a discrepancy between the research data for major brands and the stock market performance of the underlying businesses. The brand bubble hypothesis seems also to ignore the fact that about 70 percent of the leading global brands are older than 50 years. Also, the BAV study, in line with most published brand value surveys, claims that on average, brands account for about one-third of shareholder value. This leaves two-thirds of other intangible and tangible assets.

The recession that started with the sub-prime crisis in 2007 has affected spending and investments of consumers and businesses and subsequently depressed demand and prices for most goods and services. This will affect brands and their value creation. However, it would be wrong to assume that this will lead to the long-term decline of the economic importance of brands. The dynamics of economic and stock market cycles is much more complex then the BAV hypothesis suggests. The BAV survey provides some interesting insights due to the unique scale and consistency of the research. However, it does not provide clear links to economic value creation as high performance in its main criteria does not necessarily lead to financial value creation. The attempts to overlay financial data have provided some additional insights which are rather broad and reinforce long existing marketing mantras of relevance and differentiation. As such the BAV survey can be used to identify and analyze trends but not to understand and quantify the financial value of brands.

Another prominent market research approach that tries to assess brand equity is Millward Brown's BrandZ study. Interestingly, this study is like BAV, sponsored and financed by the WPP Group. Like BAV, BrandZ is a quantitative brand equity study carried out annually since 1998.[9] BrandZ interviews consumers about brands from categories in which they shop on a regular basis thereby differentiating it from BAV. Respondents evaluate the brands relative to their competitors. This, the BrandZ team believes, provides more valuable insights because respondents are knowledgeable about the brands and the category they are evaluating. The database of the BrandZ survey is large and comprises of more than 650,000 consumer interviews comparing over 25,000 brands. Through a range of statistical analyses the survey has identified several key evaluation and performance parameters. The core is the BrandDynamics pyramid which was developed by Millward Brown in 1998. The pyramid consists of five hierarchical levels. The bottom level is called *presence* and represents the familiarity interviewees have with a brand based on past trial, saliency, and knowledge of the brand's promise. The next level is *relevance* which assesses whether the brand is relevant to the respondent's needs, appropriately priced, and is in the consideration set of the respondent. The third level is *performance*. Here interviewees assess product performance and whether the brand is on their short-list. The next level up is called *advantage* and relates to the emotional or rational advantage a brand is perceived to have over other brands in the category. The top level of the pyramid is called *bonding* and refers to rational and emotional attachments to the brand that lead respondents to exclude most of the other brands in the category. Interviewees are assigned to one level of the pyramid according to their responses to a set questionnaire. The higher they are in the pyramid the stronger their relationship with and commitment to the brand. The BrandDynamics pyramid follows established marketing models that assume a hierarchical progression of consumers of a brand from awareness to some form of commitment.

The BrandDynamics pyramid shows the number of respondents that have reached each level. Millward Brown claims to have undertaken additional research to test and verify the relationship between the ranking of respondents on the pyramid and their stated purchase behavior. For each category 400 respondents were selected to complete additional questionnaires about their actual purchases 12 months after the general survey. Millward Brown claim that statistical analyses of these questionnaires support the link between the levels of the pyramids and consumer loyalty. They have developed assessments of the likelihood of consumer purchase and repurchase according to their ranking in the pyramid. According to these analyses purchasing loyalty increases at higher levels of the pyramid. There is also an increase in the proportion of consumer expenditure on that brand, within the category, as respondents ascend the pyramid or as BrandZ calls it a "strong share of wallet."[10]

BrandZ have distilled their complex survey into one key performance and benchmark metric called Brand Voltage which measures the growth potential of the brand. Brand Voltage is calculated from the bonding score and claimed purchasing data for the category. A brand with a positive voltage score has potential to increase its share from its own marketing actions and resist the actions of competitors. A brand with a negative voltage has low growth potential and is more vulnerable to the actions of other brands.[11]

The success of brand valuation and the demand for linking branding to economic value creation prompted Millward Brown in 2006 to produce a brand valuation approach based on the BrandZ study and publish it in response to the *BusinessWeek* Best Global Brands survey of the top 100 most valuable brands.[12] It follows an established three tier analysis which has become the standard of all income based approaches. First, Millward Brown establishes a company's branded earnings and allocates them to individual brands and countries of operation, based on publicly available financial data from Bloomberg, Datamonitor, and their own research. Second, they determine the portion of branded earnings that are attributable solely to the brand's equity as measured in the BrandDynamics pyramid. As a third and final step Millward Brown produces a Brand Multiple based on the Brand Momentum analysis. The value of the brand is then a simple calculation: Branded Earnings x Brand Contribution x Brand Multiple. While Millward Brown is more forthcoming in explaining the BrandZ research they are surprisingly opaque about the details of the brand valuation analysis at all levels.

The brand valuation starts with defining Branded Earnings. While Millward Brown explains that the earnings they use are specific to the brand (i.e. Coca-Cola's brand earnings exclude earnings from other brands of The Coca-Cola Company such as Fanta, Sprite, etc.) there is no specification regarding the type of earnings that are used for the calculation. From undefined brand earnings "capital charges" are subtracted. Again there is no specification regarding definition and size of capital charges. This lack of definition makes it impossible to understand the basic financial inputs that feed the valuation model. Another issue is the use of a multiples approach. The base number to which the multiplier is applied to is crucial for the valuation. Being so vague about the financial base number provides little comfort for the outcome of the valuation process. The second stage of the valuation is not much clearer. The brand earnings are obviously not what they appear to be as "only a portion of these earnings can be considered being driven by brand equity."[13] So Millward Brown determines through what they call Brand Contribution Analysis the degree to which the brand plays a role in generating earnings or a percentage of the overall brand earnings. The brand contribution then provides the earnings number to which the multiplier is applied to calculate the value of a brand. The brand contribution analysis is established through country-, market- and brand-specific customer research from the BrandZ database. It reflects the share of earnings from a product or service's most loyal consumers or users. Brand contribution is a metric made available by the BrandZ ranking that quantifies the role of the brand in driving earnings. Brand contribution reflects the share of earnings attributable to the brand alone. This metric is obtained by isolating income that comes from a brand's most loyal consumers, whose purchase decision is based on brand rather than other factors such as price. Brand contribution is calculated by using research-based consumer loyalty data from the BrandZ database. Brand contribution is presented as an index from one to five where five indicates the strongest brand contribution. It appears that brand contribution is derived from the BrandDynamics pyramid and driven by the two top levels: bonding and advantage. These levels are assumed to represent the most loyal customers with the highest expected "share of wallet." Although one can follow the assumption that respondents in the top two levels of the pyramid are more likely to be loyal customers of the brand it is not at all clear how this is supposed to relate to the brand versus non-brand factors such as price or other intangible and tangible factors. According to the latest survey from 2009 the IBM and Pepsi-Cola brands contribute the same percentage of branded earnings as both have a contribution index of 3. It easy to understand that, in the case of IBM, factors other than the brand drive the company's earnings – customer service, expertise, and global execution capabilities are factors that can be seen as less or little brand dependent. However, in the case of Pepsi-Cola it is much more difficult to follow the same logic as there is little else than the brand that drives the underlying business. With the exception of some trade promotions Pepsi is not sold at a discount compared to competing drinks products in most markets. The Pepsi brand is thus the most dominant driver of consumer choice. The analyses that have led to the brand contribution framework are not sufficiently disclosed but the comparison of the IBM and Pepsi brands demonstrate that the logic is flawed.

The final stage of the valuation process also lacks transparency. The earnings purely attributable to the brand are multiplied with a brand multiple "based on market valuations, brand growth potential and Voltage as measured by BrandDynamics."[14] Millward Brown project the brand value forward based on market valuations, the brand's risk profile, and its growth potential. Data for this step is sourced from the BrandZ database, Bloomberg, and the company's own research. Based on these inputs Millward Brown produces the brand momentum index. It is an index of a brand's short-term growth rate (1 year) relative to the average short-term growth rate of all brands in the BrandZ ranking. The brand momentum index ranges between one and 10 where 10 indicates brands with highest short-term growth potential. Brand momentum is based on three inputs: Its likelihood to gain market share and increase value; expected growth in the sector the brand operates in; and overall growth potential in a particular country and category. A brand's growth potential also depends on its current market share and awareness rates. Obviously, assessing the brand multiple is quite involved. This is fair, given its importance in determining brand values. However, no attempt is made to clarify how brand voltage, brand momentum, short term growth rates as well as all the other inputs are weighted and combined to provide the brand multiple. The results can be surprising. According to the 2009 survey, the Coca-Cola and Marlboro brands have a brand momentum of eight and nine respectively despite operating in mature and in many markets declining categories. On the other hand, Google and Intel have a brand momentum of three and two respectively despite operating in much more dynamic technology markets. Since the values are supposed to represent future cash flows this appears to be at adds with overall market and industry trends. Such results provide little confidence in the multiples that are derived from the brand momentum analysis.[15]

From a pure market research point of view, the BrandZ study provides interesting insights due to the depth of the research data. It also delivers some brand equity analyses that are useful knowledge when accessing brands. As such, it has a similar value to other brand equity research studies based on large-scale consumer research like BAV. However, similar to BAV, the results of the survey do not translate easily into a valuation approach that can assess and create understanding of the economic value of brands. The whole process lacks transparency at all stages of the valuation. Both financial and marketing inputs are unclear and misleading. Brand earnings, brand contribution, and brand multiple are insufficiently defined and explained. Despite its extensive research and data sources the BrandZ survey does not result in a convincing valuation approach. The results reflect this perfectly. In its method description Millward Brown claim that the BrandZ valuations differ positively from the high volatility of financial markets and that their "intrinsic approach" reflects the "true value rather than current market swings." However, the survey results contradict this claim as difference in year on year change of brand value ranges from value growth of 168 percent (China Merchant Bank) to a value decline of 53 percent (Bank of America). In the 2008 survey the spread was even larger ranging from a 390 percent increase of the value of the BlackBerry brand to a decline of 30 percent of the Motorola brand. Even the value of a mature and established brand such as AT&T can increase within one year by 67 percent.[16] This volatility in brand values seems in opposition to the established business wisdom that strong and powerful brands provide higher stability and predictability of cash flows. There is no question that substantial data and analyses lie behind the BrandZ survey. This however, does not translate into a credible model or approach for understanding, identifying, and assessing the value of brands. Neither the model nor the results are convincing. However, as mentioned previously, the sheer size of the survey provides some interesting insights and these need to be considered and assessed in isolation. The survey does not produce financial values that are useful and meaningful for either the marketing or financial communities. It poses more questions than it answers. As such the approach lacks credibility and confidence with respect to method and results.

The Nielsen company has also developed brand equity models that claim to link to economic value creation. The research company developed, in cooperation with Kevin Keller from the Tuck School of Business, a brand equity index based on research on more than 2,400 brands. The brand equity score is calculated based on interviewees' response to questions regarding favorability, recommendation, and willingness to pay a premium price. The index scores range from one to 10, the latter represents the maximum score attainable. The approach is relatively simple and contains the main brand equity components. The company claims that it can link the results to consumer loyalty, but it does not provide an explicit link to financial results. Nielsen has also tried to stretch its brand equity thinking to brand valuation. Its model assesses the economic value of a brand based on sales data. The annual sales of a brand are multiplied with a brand strength factor expressed as a percentage. Brand strength is assessed according to four core indicators.

These indicators are given different weighting totaling 100 percent. The first, market attractiveness, has a weighting of 15 percent. This indicator assesses the attractiveness of the market in which the brand operates according to volume and growth prospects. The second indicator is the brand's acceptance within the market with a weighting of 35 percent. This indicator looks at how the brand performs in its market, its existing market share, and share growth in value terms. The third indicator is consumer acceptance which has the highest weighting of 40 percent. Consumer acceptance is measured through brand awareness and brand consideration. The fourth indicator is distribution with a weighting of 10 percent. It measures the distribution coverage and availability of the brand. The derived percentage is applied to normalized annual revenues of the brand. The result is called the brand strength profit. It is multiplied with a discount factor representing average market return to calculate the value of the brand. This calculation assumes an unlimited life span of the brand as well as a constant sales return.[17]

The Nielsen approach is relatively simple and can be executed with a data set that is easily available in most companies. It is, however, overly simplistic and lacks some key elements. The financial assumptions are probably the hardest to accept. Using a brand strength assessment to derive the profitability of a brand does not fit with any established

34

financial principles and is therefore an assumption that would require substantial validation. It is not an assumption that any financially literate person would find easily acceptable. The approach does not differentiate between the brand and other business assets. The assumption must be that the brand strength profit represents the financial return of the brand and everything else refers to other costs and returns from other business assets. This is a questionable assumption. The simplistic forecasting is out of line with common financial practice. The brand strength indicators are basic but include some of the important metrics such as market share, awareness, consideration, and distribution. How they are derived and weighted is unclear and therefore hard to assess. The financial approach is questionable and there is no causal link between marketing and finance. Overall, the Nielsen approach is not suitable to assess the economic value of brands.

The Ipsos Group has also developed a brand equity approach based on their research experience and capabilities. Their "measure of brand equity uses a handful of standardized attitude measures that are generalizable across brands, business sectors, and markets. These measures have been derived from a comprehensive study of 200 different brands from 40 different product and service categories, comprising over 12,000 consumer interviews for over 200,000 individual brand assessments."[18] Ipsos' brand equity model is called "Brand Health" and is built on three main factors: Brand equity perceptions; consumer involvement with the category; and price/value perceptions. These measures are derived based on a series of standard rating scales.

Each factor is composed of several dimensions. Brand equity perceptions comprise familiarity, uniqueness, relevance, popularity, and quality. Involvement reflects consumers' reported sensitivity to differences between brands, how much they matter in their specific category, and how easily they can be substituted. Price represents the perceived price/value relationship. The three factors have been correlated with a brand health assessment comprising reported brand loyalty, commitment, purchase intent ratings, and price sensitivity as well as market share and to 5-year trends in share and profitability. Ipsos also ran a survey to develop understanding and identification of the drivers of brand equity. By far the most important driver of brand equity was product performance. The following factors were packaging, visual identity (logo, feel, artwork), and brand name. Each of them had a similar impact. Advertising was the fifth most important factor but had a relatively minor impact. The Ipsos model comprises the key elements found in most of the sophisticated brand equity models. However, the driver analysis shows some limitations as, for example, product performance is difficult to measure for many packaged goods, products such as soft drinks and snacks. The other brand equity drivers are very closely interrelated and hard to separate. Brand name, visual identity, and packaging have a very similar correlation which may indicate that they have been perceived as communicating the same message as they all visually represent the brand. In the case of packaged goods, the product's name, logo, and packaging will all identify the brand and its message. The driver analysis appears therefore limited. Overall, the Ipsos model covers the main components of brand equity but does not link into financial value creation. As such, it is not suitable for assessing the economic value of brands.[19]

Another variation of the research-based brand equity approach has been developed by PricewaterhouseCoopers (PwC). The core concept is the price premium that consumers are willing to pay over and above the lowest cost also known as the "willingness to pay" (WTP). PwC regard this metric as the ultimate value assessment for brands. It rests on the established research technique called conjoint or "trade-off" analysis which is employed in product development and pricing research. Consumers choose between different options of offers and price levels. The result is the preference to pay relatively more than the cheapest offer in the set. This PwC believes represents an expression of consumer preference and thus a trusted economic measure. The approach is limited by its focus on price premium and the lack of a resulting economic or financial value. According to the WTP logic, the higher the price premium consumers are willing to pay the higher the absolute value. However, price differentials in a category can easily blur and the difference in options may be marginal. There is also the behavioral impact of increasing price and declining relevance. An optimal price is not necessarily the highest chargeable price but the balance between price and volume. Also conjoint studies tend to work best for direct material differences but much less or not at all for soft image aspects and other variables that influence the purchase but are harder to imagine for interviewees in a research situation. The comparison of the options tends to be driven by the hard tangible aspects such as price and product functions. In the case of a car this could be engine size, warranties, and extras such as leather seats and alloy wheels. However, it is harder to add softer and emotional aspects into the options such as cool, stylish, or safe. In addition, aspects such as dealer network, point of sale influence by the sales representative are other aspects that are difficult to include in such an approach. Therefore, these studies work with a limited set of tangible or hard attributes neglecting the softer elements of consumer choice. They underestimate the impact of emotional factors which are fundamental in understanding the value creation of brands. In addition, WTP provides a preference metric but not a financial value for the brand.[20]

A rather simple and easily understandable brand equity measurement is the net promoter score introduced by Frederick Reichheld from Bain & Co.[21] Companies obtain their Net Promoter Score by registering customers' responses to a single question on a 0–10 rating scale. For example, "How likely is it that you would recommend our company to a friend or colleague?" Based on their responses, customers can be categorized into one of three groups: promoters (9–10 rating); passives (7–8 rating); and detractors (0–6 rating). The percentage of detractors is then subtracted from the percentage of promoters to obtain a Net Promoter score. A score of 75 percent or above is considered quite high. Although the approach follows familiar and established customer satisfaction surveys it became popular due to its simplicity. Beyond the publicity the approach does not offer much more than traditional customer satisfaction surveys as respondents are likely to answer satisfaction and recommendation in a similar fashion. Many satisfaction surveys use several questions including satisfaction and recommendation statements to avoid survey dependence on the result of one question. The main and obvious limitation of the net promoter approach is the lack of insights and identification of causal relationships which seriously limits its use. It provides little insight into what drives the financial performance of a business or of what contributes to the Net Promoter score. It may be correlated with some latent construct of brand equity but, in the end, the only reasonable interpretation is to take the measure at face value. It is simply the stated likelihood that the survey respondent will recommend your brand to others. As such it is a very basic tracking device. It is unsuitable for assessing brand equity and the economic value of brands as it does not link directly into either.

The main achievement of brand equity has been to distill and develop, out of the data pool of market research, economically relevant concepts and metrics. They have helped to provide structure and economic logic to the marketing view of the value creation of brands in particular with respect to purchase intent and behavior as well as loyalty. However, the logic of many equity models rests on proprietary research and insights which are not disclosed. Without understanding and verification of the underlying research and assumptions made, many of these models are difficult to understand and follow. Although there is a positive claim as to the depth of data, the scope of surveys, and the statistical analyses, there is a lack of disclosure around the assumptions that make these models work. This is not surprising as most agencies want to exploit their models commercially to sell their clients market research programs. Many of these models are also based on established market research surveys which had to be statistically reengineered to provide a model fit with some statistical relevance. Traditionally, the focus of most market research has been on assessing the impact of media communications which limits the overall point of view on the value creation of brands. In general, most models fall victim to having to balance too many variables, established question-naire designs, and research methods into a statistically cohesive model. While the resulting models may produce statistically relevant results they are limited by the data input. The acknowledgement of one of the models, that only 25 percent of market value was supposedly explained by brand factors from market research studies and 55 percent from financial data, shows the lack of linkage between the research-based brand equity models and relevant financial outcomes. The lack of inte-grating financial and marketing analyses, therefore, produces limited results.

Brand equity models have added a long-term view on brand value as a balance to short-term sales impacts of marketing initiatives. As such, they have provided crucial building blocks for the economic assess-ment of brands. However, all brand equity models grapple with their ambition to explain economic and ultimately financial outcomes. The financial term "equity" is used to demonstrate the economic relevance of the different research approaches. They are, therefore, in a difficult position as they imply that they can explain economic outcomes but do not follow through with a credible financial model. Many equity models have completed some type of share price or profitability corre-lation to claim the validity of their approaches. These, however, tend to be limited by the time periods they cover and are not integrated parts of the models but add on justifications. Those equity models that have integrated a financial module into their approach have so far not delivered convincing results. The joint venture between Y&R's BAV and Stern Stewart lasted only a couple of years and the BrandZ's financial output is confused and difficult to reconcile. There is a clear imbalance between the sophistication that goes into the market research modules and the simplicity of the financial analyses. Within these models the financial analysis is not a core component of the approach but an add-on designed to sell marketing to financially focused audiences. This is reflected in the quality of the brand valuation approaches and results. The brand equity models provide the marketing data and metrics that are necessary to understand and assess the economic value of brands. They are, however, only one side of the equation. A matching financial analysis is required to provide a comprehensive brand valuation approach.

CHAPTER 5

FINANCIAL APPROACHES TO VALUING BRANDS

The financial community seriously woke up to the importance of intangibles and brands in the 1980s when some large financial transactions were completed on the back of well-established brand portfolios. The leveraged buy out of RJR Nabisco, a US consumer goods business with a diverse portfolio of tobacco and food brands, by KKR, a leading US based leveraged buyout firm, for US$31 billion in 1989 was a landmark transaction based on the steady cash flows of the target company's brand portfolio. It remained the largest leverage buy-out until November 2006 when the same group joined the US$33 billion buyout of US hospital chain HCA.[1] Also, in the 1980s a number of significant M&A transactions emerged involving companies with strong brands such as Nestlé buying Rowntree for UK£2.8 billion (five times its book value) and Philip Morris acquiring Kraft General Foods for US$12.9 billion (six times its book value) with about 90 percent of the value represented by the company's brand portfolio.[2] These transactions did not only show that intangibles such as brands are valuable business assets they also highlighted the increasing value gap between companies' book and market values. In the 1980s the price to tangible book value of the S&P500 started its long-term ascent. Within the decade the ratio more than doubled from 1.1 to 2.6. Even during 2008/9, one of the worst bear markets in history, that ratio did not drop below 2.7 meaning that investors assumed that intangible assets accounted for about 63 percent of shareholder value.[3] This gap between book and stock market value showed that investors were paying little attention to the balance sheet and recognized the value of intangibles including brands, R&D, distribution rights, and management know-how. As long as this gap was relatively small the financial community did not regard it as a major issue. If a company acquired another company for a price that exceeded the book value of the business the difference between the purchase price and the book value was called goodwill and written off against reserves. This was not a big issue as long as the goodwill portion was minor and could comfortably be written off without a major impact on the balance sheet. However, in particular cases where the target company owned strong brands the goodwill portion increased dramatically to a level when a write-off was seriously damaging the balance sheet of the acquiring company. The accounting treatment of goodwill was clearly out of sync with economic reality. This sparked the accounting debate and subsequent changes in the accounting treatment of goodwill which are discussed in Chapter 8. The financial approaches to brand valuation can be grouped into three categories: cost; market; and income based approaches.

Cost-based approaches

Cost-based approaches value an asset according to the acquisition cost of the asset. There are two types of cost-based approaches. The first one is the original cost approach which values assets based on their original acquisition costs. In the case of a brand, the original cost value would be the sum of all directly identifiable investments that were made into the brand including brand development, design, trade mark registration and maintenance, advertising, and corporate identity management. The approach is simple and, if accurate documentation exits, easy to implement. While historic costs may be interesting for an ROI assessment they do not provide a suitable valuation approach for brands as there is no clear relationship between historic investments in a brand and the economic benefit they generate. For example, GM has invested a lot of money in brands such as Pontiac, Oldsmobile, and Saturn. Today these brands are defunct or in the process of being discontinued. On the other hand, the value of the Red Bull brand will exceed the value of its investments. The whole purpose of brands as assets is that they create much more value than the monetary investment they require. An important investment in the brand is the concept and overall brand idea which is independent of costs as it depends on the creativity of its development. In addition, it is for most established brands impossible to track all past investments that were made into the brand. For leading brands such as Coca-Cola, Kellogg's, or GE it will be impossible to trace all the investments that were made into these brands. However, the main reason why the historic cost approach is not suitable for brands is the fact that there is little relationship between the money that is invested in a brand and its economic value creation.

Replacement cost approach

The other and more relevant cost approach is the replacement cost approach that values assets based on what it would cost to replace them if they were acquired or recreated today. Replacement costs may be determined either by finding current prices for assets, or by applying an inflation factor to the original cost. The replacement cost approach is economically more relevant as it represents the actual costs required to obtain a certain asset. The approach can be applicable for the valuation of assets for which current values are easily available and for which the application of replacement makes sense such as a building. The replacement cost is only suitable for valuing a brand if it has not been used in the market or its awareness level is negligible when its value equals its development and registration costs. For actively used brands this approach is unsuitable as there is no meaningful relationship between the cost of establishing a brand and its economic value. Established brands such as Coca-Cola, Nivea, or Sony would be impossible to replace due to their position in the market place.

For fair-value determinations of intangible assets, using a cost-oriented method plays a subordinate role. It is typically used to value assets to which no cash flows can be assigned. The cost approach is often used to value internally developed software. Thereby the costs that would have to be incurred in order to produce an exact duplicate of the asset (reproduction costs) are considered. Alternatively, it is possible to base the valuation on the estimated costs required to produce an asset with an equivalent benefit (replacement costs). Cost-based approaches are not suitable for valuing brands as there is no clear relationship between the cost of establishing and maintaining the brand and its economic value creation. Investing a lot of money in a brand does not guarantee economic success as the majority of new product launches demonstrates. Positively, it is the nature of effective branding that the returns achieved are far higher than the investments made.

Market value approaches

The market value approach works on the premise that an asset can be valued by looking at the market price of comparable assets. In the case of company valuations this can be companies quoted on the stock market or companies that have been subject to an acquisition. The asset price is assessed on the basis of a multiple of annual revenue or profits (e.g. EBIT, EBITDA, net profit) of the purchase price or stock market value. This valuation technique is widely used in financial transactions. The relationship between the share price and company earnings, also called P/E ratios, is commonly used to assess and compare the value of companies. Despite all the sophistication in financial modeling value multiples are used in most M&A transactions. The market value approach benefits from the perceived factual objectivity of prices that have been paid for comparable assets. However, the key issue of this approach is comparability. In order for this approach to work there needs to be a significant number of comparable transactions or quoted companies to derive a meaningful value. While it is difficult for most companies to find truly comparable businesses it is in most cases impossible to establish for brands. The value of companies with strong brands always includes additional assets. Therefore, comparable values do not lend themselves to the valuation of brands. In addition, the number of pure brand transactions is very small and often involves cases where the underlying business has collapsed. An example would be Woolworth's in the UK, when the business went into reccivership the brand was sold on its own to an Internet retailer. In such cases the multiples tend to be useless. The market approach does not work for the brand as they are and should not be comparable. The whole purpose of brands is to be different and unique. Take the example of the Coca-Cola and Pepsi-Cola brands. The underlying businesses are probably as close as is possible to find. Their products are nearly identical, they target the same markets and audiences, they have similar distribution approaches and systems, and they charge similar prices for their products. Without the brands their products would be indistinguishable. Their brands however, are very different with respect to image and value creation. Coca-Cola is the original market leading cola brand and Pepsi is the eternal challenger. The Coca-Cola brand has a larger market share and Coca-Cola's average operating margin over the last five years was about 8 percent greater than that of Pepsi-Cola's. According to *BusinessWeek*'s Best Global Brands survey the Coca-Cola brand is valued as a multiple of annual brand sales of about 3.4 times versus the Pepsi-Cola brand that is valued at a sales multiple of 2.2.[4] The Coca-Cola brand has a strong global footprint while the Pepsi brand is much more focused on the US market. The example of the Coca-Cola and

Pepsi-Cola brands demonstrates that even in very comparable businesses brands are not comparable. As a result, the market approach is not suitable for valuing brands due to the lack of comparable transactions and the unique nature of brands. If comparable transactions and brand values are available then they should be used as a cross-check, but as a main valuation approach market comparables are not suitable for valuing brands.

Most accounting standards recommend the market approach as the first option for valuing intangible assets. However, since there is neither a liquid market for most intangibles nor suitable comparables the market approach is not used frequently in accounting practice. The most recent fair value debate acknowledges that intangible assets tend to be unique and situation specific. This has led to accounting practice focusing on the income approach for the balance sheet recognition of intangible assets.

Income approach

The income approach values an asset as the net present value (NPV) of the cash flows it is estimated to accrue during its economic life. It is the most widely accepted approach and in line with current corporate finance theory. The income approach is therefore the most widely used method for valuing intangibles including brands. There are several versions of the income approach. The main difference is how the asset specific earnings and discount rate are identified and calculated. There are three income approach methods.

The first, the multi-period excess earnings method, is based on the assumption that cash flows can only be generated from an intangible asset in conjunction with other tangible or intangible assets. In order to separate the intangible asset to be valued, payments for the supporting assets are considered as contributory asset charges. The approach identifies returns for all the other assets which are subtracted in addition to the operating costs from the overall revenue stream. The unidentified returns are then assumed to accrue to the intangible asset to be valued. Accounting firms often use this approach to value technologies and customer relations. The difficulty with this approach lies in the assumed returns and charges for the other assets. While it is relatively easy to find returns for tangible assets such as office and factory buildings, it is much harder to identify the return of specific intangibles such as customer lists and brands. Accounting firms have derived lists of fictitious charges for such assets. However, the validity of some these returns can be questioned. This approach is mainly driven by the need to find values for a wide range of intangibles to be recognized on the balance sheet in the course of a purchase price allocation.

The second income approach for valuing an intangible asset is the incremental cash flow method. This method determines the difference between the cash flows of the company with the relevant intangible asset and a fictitious company without this asset. The difference represents the additional cash flow related to the intangible asset, and discounting this as the asset specific capitalization leads to its fair value. This approach is a simpler version of the previous one as it only makes assumptions about the cash flow of the intangible asset to be valued and not the other intangibles in the business. It works on the principle of exclusion by assuming all earnings that are not attributable to the specific intangible asset valued represent the return of the other business assets. This approach is mostly applied in the form of a profit-split approach, where after remunerating the capital employed in the business the remainder is split between the intangible asset valued and the other intangible assets. This approach is used by many consulting firms, such as Interbrand and Millward Brown Optimor that specialize in valuing brands. The validity of this approach very much depends on the quality of the method used for identifying the earnings attributable to all intangibles as well as to the specific intangible, i.e. the brand. This approach will be discussed in more detail later.

Another version of the incremental cash flow method is the price premium approach. It is based on the premise that brands can command a price premium over and above non-branded or generic offers. The approach compares the revenues of the branded offer with a generic product and calculates the NPV of the future cash flows stemming from this price differential. As previously noted, there are also market research models that base their brand assessment mainly on the willingness of consumers to purchase at a premium. The price-premium approach has been used by many consulting firms such as McKinsey and PricewaterhouseCoopers. The approach is flawed as it focuses on the price premium as the only source of brand value and the assumption that there are comparable branded products and services sold in the market. In reality there are only a very small number of categories in which generic and branding products are sold in competition, for example, petrol, lubricants, and pharmaceuticals. The pharmaceutical industry and some commodity based industries such as lubricants are probably the only sectors where generic products have some significance. Otherwise unbranded generic offers do not exist as all products and services are branded. Even "own label" products offered by supermarkets have become brands in their own rights. Some supermarkets have applied very sophisticated branding around their products. In the UK, some supermarkets offer premium ranges of their own label products at a price premium over some established brands. Creating a difference between a brand and a generic offer has become irrelevant – the generic simply does not exist. This makes the assessment of price premium very difficult. At best one can compare premium brands with the cheapest brands in the market. Even that approach will be very difficult as in most cases brands do not provide the same offer. The price premium of a Rolls-Royce Phantom or an S Class Mercedes depends on the benchmark. It will be huge in comparison to a Tata Nano or a Nissan Micra but not very meaningful for assessing the value of these brands. In fact many mass-market brands create more value than premium brands. The value of the Toyota brand is more than seven times that of the Porsche brand. In many categories the price differential between brands is minor. For example, consider televisions where there are several brands with very similar price points in different product and price categories. In telecommunication and financial services, pricing differentials are hard to identify and often meaningless as they change with different bundled offers. As a result a brand may have a price premium in one offer but not in another. Premium pricing is an important value driver for certain brands in particular in the luxury goods category. It is, however, not the only value driver for the majority of brands as volume, frequency of purchase, and supporting cost structures tend to be equally relevant for their value creation. The premium price approach ignores key value drivers and places too much emphasis on one value driver. While a price premium is an important indicator of the strength of a brand it does not provide a sufficient basis for a valuation of the brand. Price premium is one of several assessment criteria but not a valid brand valuation approach.

A third and frequently used method for valuing intangible assets is the relief from royalty method. This method is typically employed for the valuation of brands and patents. It is based on the fundamental premise that an external third party would be prepared to pay a license fee for the use of a brand or a patent that it does not own. The value of the intangible asset is then calculated as the present value of the saved license payments. The approach is popular with accounting firms and some specialized brand valuation consultancies due to its simplicity and perceived objectivity. However, the approach is really another version of valuing intangible assets by comparison. This is a significant drawback of this approach as it relies on the comparability of royalty rates. However, relative to other comparables, such as transactions, there is much more data available on royalty rates. The difficulty arises when applying comparable royalties due to comparability and clarity of what the royalty rate encompasses. Most royalty agreements are not publicly disclosed and often bundle several intangibles into one royalty rate. Also, many licensing rates that are part of franchise agreements are linked to other charges such as the requirement to purchase certain raw materials at fixed prices exclusively from the licensor. In such situations the pure license fee does not represent the total return the licensor receives for licensing the intangible asset. These hidden returns can only be identified by analyzing the entire agreement. Most of these agreements are secretive and not publicly available. Brand licensing rates can range from less than 1 percent to more than 20 percent of revenues. Even in the same category, licensing rates can vary dramatically by geography and application. For example, the royalty rate for a fashion brand will differ between its use in sunglasses and perfumes. It will also vary by geography. The same brand will command a different royalty in the US than in China. In telecommunications, for example, royalty rates can range from 2 to 8 percent.[5] The diversity of rates according to different markets makes the royalty relief method difficult to apply. The royalties approach only works if a significant number of comparable rates can be identified. This is not often the case in particular when dealing with brand licenses. The approach faces the same comparability issue as the market approach. The uniqueness of brands makes comparability difficult. The royalty relief method can also lead to brands being undervalued as the royalty represents only the brand value to the licensor but not the licencee. The approach also fails to deliver insight into the value creation of the specific brand as it relies on the rate from another brand. Therefore it does not deliver reliable brand valuations and should not be used as the primary valuation approach for valuing brands. The royalty relief approach can be useful to cross-check for other more brand-specific valuation approaches as it provides a third party view on the value of a brand license in the same industry.

Most of the traditional income approaches have been developed by financial professionals and are mainly focused on the financial component of valuing intangible assets and brands. It has been predominantly the accounting profession that has been active in this field as it has to deal with intangible assets on balance sheets which emerged from the purchase price allocations and subsequent impairment tests stipulated by all the relevant accounting rules around the world. In developing valuation techniques for intangibles, they have extended and adjusted their established valuation methods. As the majority of valuations of intangible assets performed by accounting firms focus on establishing a financial value, mainly for balance sheet recognition, the valuation approaches are more concerned with the mechanics of the calculation than a deep understanding of the underlying assets. The objective of the purchase price allocation valuations is to split and allocate a given goodwill value that has emerged from a transaction into fair values for the individual intangible assets. The valuations are therefore performed top down from an already determined financial value. The focus is on the relative value of each intangible asset. The purpose of the valuation is therefore not to understand the value of each of the intangibles to derive an overall value for these assets, but to allocate a given overall asset value to different intangible asset classes as required by the accounting standards. This explains why accounting valuations are more concerned with the financial and numeric mechanics of intangible asset valuations. From an accounting perspective this is perfectly fine and practical. It may also work for some technical intangibles such as software licenses but it is certainly not suitable for the valuation of brands. This has to a certain extent been acknowledged by the accounting profession. The current fair value debate about intangible assets suggests that due to the unique nature of many intangible assets such as brands the conventional comparables focused approaches are insufficient and asset specific techniques need to be used to assess a fair value of these assets. In a discussion paper of fair value the IVSC, an international accounting standards body, acknowledges the existence of different assets, i.e. non-comparable intangible assets such as brands, that they suggest should be valued according to the specific earnings stream they create.[6]

CHAPTER 6

INTEGRATING FINANCE AND MARKETING: ECONOMIC USE METHOD

The purely market research and financially focused methods deliver unsatisfactory results for assessing the economic value of brands because they are either weak on the marketing or financial understanding. As a result, new valuation approaches emerged that integrate financial and marketing analyses into one valuation approach. This is referred to as the "economic use" method. This method values the brand as an integral part of a company and focuses on the added value the brand provides to the underlying business. This approach emerged due to a need to go beyond the mechanics of calculating a financial value to understand and manage the value creation of brands. This requires a detailed understanding and valuation of the specific value creation of a brand. There are several consulting firms that have developed their version of the economic use approach including Interbrand, Brand Finance, and Millward Brown.

One of the most famous economic use approaches was developed by Interbrand – a consulting company that pioneered brand valuation in the late 1980s. The initial approach was developed for financial purposes to help companies to recognize the value of their brands on the balance sheet. The model was a relatively simple multiples approach. The basis for determining the earnings attributable to the brand was the operating profit of the business using the brand. Taxes and a charge for the capital employed in the business were subtracted from the operating profit to derive brand earnings. The multiplier was determined through a brand strength assessment. The strength of a brand was assessed on a scale of 0–10. The extreme ends of the scale represented theoretical concepts. A completely unknown brand would receive a score of 0 while a notionally perfect brand would receive a score of 100. A brand with a brand strength score of 0 would have a multiple of 0 and thus no value. A brand with a score of 100 would receive a multiple of 20 which was derived from P/E (Price/Earnings) multiples of quoted companies with strong brands. The multiples between the two extremes are determined through an "S" shaped curve representing the relationship between brand strength and brand value, i.e., the stronger the brand the higher the value and vice-versa. The brand strength is determined according to seven factors. Each factor has a different maximum weight with the sum of all factors adding up to 100. The factors and their weighting are as follows:

1. *Leadership* (25/100)
   This factor assesses the degree to which a brand influences the market it operates in. Indicators are setting price points, command distribution, and being resistant against competitive pressures.

2. *Stability* (15/100)
   This factor refers to consumer loyalty and whether the brand has become the "fabric" of the market it operates in.

3. *Market* (10/100)
   This factor refers to the market the brand operates in. This is assessed according to growth rates, barriers to entry, and risk of structural change.

4. *Internationality* (25/100)
   This factor looks at the geographic spread of the brand based on the assumption that the more markets and cultures the brand can penetrate the more valuable it is.

5. *Trend* (10/100)
   This factor measures the ability of a brand to stay contemporary and relevant in its markets.

6. *Support* (10/100)
   This factor assesses the amount of marketing spend as well as the management of the contents of a brand.

7. *Protection* (5/100)
   This factor assesses how well the legal protection is managed including trademark registration and management.[1]

The brand strength model has been the most consistent element of Interbrand's brand valuation approach. Although the firm has adjusted its valuation approach over the years, the principles of the brand strength model remained mainly unchanged.[2] The firm made two significant changes to its valuation approach. First, it switched from a multiples approach to a NPV calculation of brand specific earnings. Second, it introduced a profit-split element called "role of branding" that separated the earnings attributable to the brand from the earnings of the other intangibles.[3] The switch from a multiples approach to a NPV calculation resulted in the brand strength model being applied to the discount rate instead of a P/E multiple. The model assumes that the strongest possible brand receives a score of 100 and has a risk profile similar to government bonds. The discount rate changes according to the strength of the brand meaning that the weaker the brand the higher the discount rate and vice-versa.[4] Through these adjustments Interbrand has defined the main elements of the economic use approach that values a brand in the context of owner and user. This valuation approach comprises three key elements: Financial forecasting of intangible earnings; identification and separation of the earnings attributable to the brand; and a brand strength assessment to determine a brand specific discount rate. The steps in detail are as follows:

1. *Financial forecasting*: The firm forecasts the current and future revenue specifically attributable to the branded products. It then subtracts operating costs, taxes, and a charge to the brand's profit for capital employed to derive the economic earnings.
2. *Role of brand analysis*: Here Interbrand assesses which part of the economic earnings is attributable specifically to the brand. The role of brand measures how the brand influences customer demand at the point of purchase. This is applied to the economic earnings to arrive at Branded Earnings. The approach is proprietary and not disclosed in further detail.
3. *Brand strength analysis*: The seven brand strength factors determine the discount rate which is used to calculate the NPV of the brand specific earnings.

Based on these three steps Interbrand calculates brand value as the NPV of the forecast brand earnings.[5]

Another firm that has developed a similar economic use approach is Brand Finance. Their approach is very similar to that of Interbrand (which is not surprising as the founder previously worked for Interbrand) but differs in some aspects in the brand analyses. The value of a brand is calculated as NPV of future expected earnings attributable to the brand. Brand Finance's valuation methodology follows the following steps:

1. *Financial forecasting*
   Brand Finance prepares a 5-year revenue forecast based on company data, analyst estimates, and overall macroeconomic data such GDP growth. The company also identifies a final growth rate for the perpetuity calculation.

2. *Brand specific earnings*
   For identifying the brand specific earnings Brand Finance uses the royalty relief method. Based on publicly available data, it identifies and selects royalty rates from brands that are assumed to be comparable to the brand being valued. From these comparable royalty rates it derives a fictitious licensing rate that is applied to the revenue forecast to derive the brand earnings forecast. The main flaw here is the assumed comparability (discussed earlier). In order to create value, brands need to be different and therefore, should not be comparable.

3. *Brand rating*
   Similar to Interbrand, Brand Finance measure the strength of a brand on a 0–100 rating scale according to a number of attributes such as brand presence, emotional connection, market share, and profitability. The brand rating benchmarks the strength, risk, and future potential of a brand relative to its competitors on a scale ranging from AAA to D. The rating results are defined in the following way:

   – AAA Extremely strong
   – AA Very strong
   – A Strong
   – BBB-B Average
   – CCC-C Weak
   – DDD-D Failing

The brand rating is converted into a brand beta, which takes additional factors into consideration such as geographic presence and reputation that are beyond the rating attributes. The brand beta determines the discount rate that is applied to the future brand earnings. The value of the brand is the net present value of the forecast brand earnings.[6] The Brand Finance approach relies on comparable royalties to derive the brand specific profits. However, in many categories royalties can vary more than 100 percent making the final selection very judgmental.

Another version of the economic use approach is provided by Millward Brown based on the BrandZ brand equity study. The approach has been discussed previously.

While these are the main internationally established and used brand valuation approaches there many more variations on the same themes. Several studies have identified more than 40 brand valuation approaches.[7] While in principal rather similar they all claim to use proprietary research analysis tools to determine the value of brands.

The brand valuation methodologies of Interband, Brand Finance, and Millward Brown have become prominent due to the brand value rankings these firms publish on an annual basis. Although there are many other versions of the economic use approach they tend to follow similar frameworks. The ranking surveys published by the brand consulting firms show that the different methods produce rather different results for the same brands (see Table 6.1).

TABLE 6.1 **Brand value comparison**

Brand value in $ million	Interbrand	Millward Brown	BrandFinance
Coca-Cola	68,734	67,625	32,728
IBM	60,211	66,662	31,530
GE	47,777	59,793	26,654
Nokia	34,864	35,163	19,889
Apple	15,433	63,113	13,648
McDonald's	32,275	66,575	20,003
HSBC	10,510	19,079	25,364
American Express	14,971	14,963	9,944
Google	31,980	100,039	29,261
Nike	13,179	11,999	14,583

Sources: Best Global Brands (2009) BrandZ Top 100, 2009; Global 500, 2009.

While there are occasional similarities in the values at least between two of the firms there are staggering differences in the value of established brands such as IBM and McDonald's. The value differences are even more dramatic with respect to the annual value changes. This has caused considerable confusion and has given the impression that valuing brands is a rather arbitrary affair. The cause is not helped by the fact that many agencies use proprietary tools based on their own research and experience for their brand specific analyses. The lack of disclosure of the valuation inputs and assumptions is responsible for the differences in brand values these models produce. Neither the financial nor the marketing inputs are sufficiently disclosed to allow a reconciliation of the brand values published in the surveys of these agencies. This is confirmed by a study published by a German magazine in 2004. The publication asked nine agencies offering brand valuations to value the brand of a fictitious petrol retailing chain. This included prominent brand valuation firms such as Interbrand and leading accounting firms such as PwC and KPMG. The agencies were given the same data and information and were asked to use their approaches to come up with a brand value for the fictional retail petrol company called Tank AG. The results showed dramatic differences in values ranging between €173 million and €958 million representing a difference of 454 percent.[8] This study also confirms that due to the lack of disclosure and the use of "proprietory" models, the brand values cannot be compared or assessed. It would however, be unfair and counter productive to dismiss brand valuation as a discipline due to the differences in approaches and valuation results. Personal experience has shown that brand valuation can deliver significant strategic insights and guidance on brand and business strategy. Knowing how brands create value is very useful in understanding business and stock market performances of companies. It would be wise to be more realistic regarding the expectations toward brand valuation.

All financial valuations are based on a set of assumptions at a particular point in time. NPV valuations represent the cash flows that an asset is expected to generate during its economic life.[9] The share price targets for the next 12 months for a stable branded business such as The Coca-Cola Company from 11 analysts covering the company had a variance of about 30 percent as of 31 August 2009.[10] This demonstrates that even analysts that spend their careers analyzing and valuing this company and its peers differ significantly in their valuations. The point here is not to question the validity of valuation in general and the discounted cash flow (DCF) approach in particular. DCF is the dominant and most widely used approach for valuing nearly all assets. It is the foundation and guiding valuation principle for corporate finance theory, capital markets, and businesses. Although DCF is the professional asset valuation approach it is not a precise science. The period 2008/9 has proven how a change in circumstances can affect valuation most notably in capital markets. As brand valuation is a derivative of business valuation the same issues apply. Although all NPV valuations based on the DCF approach use the same principles and underlying model the results can differ dramatically. This is due to the amount of assumptions that need to be made for such valuations. This includes revenue growth rates, profit margins, investment requirements, capital structure, and discount rate to name a few. Due to different inputs for these items valuations can vary substantially despite using the same valuation approach. This means the judgment about the valuation inputs has a significant impact on the outcome and validity of the valuation. In order to assess different valuations one needs to understand the underlying assumptions. The ultimate test for the validity of a valuation is the market test or exchange value of an asset in a transaction between two parties. In the case of capital market predictions about asset valuations, share prices are constantly validated due to the liquidity of these markets. Unfortunately, for brands such a market does not exist. Their value is mostly wrapped up with other assets. A direct market validation of brand values is therefore not possible. However, brand value can be compared to shareholder value as well as the value of other intangibles. These ratios provide some cross and reasonability checks. Most importantly, the consulting firms that publish the league tables need to improve disclosure about their models and assumptions. This would very quickly explain the valuation difference between different approaches.

The need to find more common ground and clarity in valuing brands has prompted several initiatives. The German standardization office Deutsches Institut für Normung (DIN) has initiated a work group for creating an ISO standard for brand valuation.[11] Such a standard already exists for market research. DIN believes that an ISO standard would provide some transparency and quality standards that would lift the reputation of the discipline and would make the results of brand valuation more reliable. Although many countries are participating in the effort, there are some prominent absentees most notably the US, Russia, and the Latin American countries. A wide-range of constituencies has been involved including brand consulting firms, accounting firms, law firms, and market research companies. Given the diversity of backgrounds and approaches many of them offer it will be a difficult task to get a meaningful consensus. A realistic outcome would be a set of guidelines that clarify approach, data input, and assumptions of a brand valuation that enable an outside party to understand the individual valuation steps as well as the valuation results. Additionally, German representatives from several accounting, brand consulting, and market research firms engaged in the valuation of brands have formed a brand valuation forum that published 10 principles of monetary brand valuation. They stipulate that a brand should be valued as NPV of future brand earnings where the brand specific earnings and risks should be identified through a set of parameters.[12]

CHAPTER 7

BRAND VALUATION BEST PRACTICE APPROACH

Out of current brand valuation theory and practice, some consensus on brand valuation emerges. This has been distilled into a tested and recommended brand valuation framework and will be described. The review of the different approaches to brand valuation demonstrates that the approach needs to integrate marketing and financial analyses without sacrificing one to the other. In line with corporate finance theory, as well as capital market and industry practice, the main valuation approach should be a NPV of future expected brand earnings. The valuation approach needs to focus on the specific value creation of the brand to be assessed. The use of comparables including royalties, as well as transactions, should be confined to cross-check analyses and not constitute the main approach. Cost approaches are only appropriate in situations where the brand has not yet been used, or has had no measurable impact on the market. This section develops, out of empirical experience and the review of the currently used methods, a best-practice approach to brand valuation. The recommended valuation approach should comprise five key steps as shown in Figure 7.1.

Step 1: Market segmentation

Most brands operate in more than one market segment which is reflected in their value creation. For example brands such as GE, Siemens, and Samsung sell a wide range of products to very different customer groups. The Samsung brand sells TVs to consumer markets around the world as well as memory chips to computer and mobile phone manufacturers. The same brand affects the different customer groups to a different degree with a different financial result. For example the Samsung brand may have a higher impact on the purchase decision of a television but the impact of the Samsung brand

Step 1: Market Segmentation	Step 2: Financial Analysis	Step 3: Brand Impact	Step 4: Discount Rate	Step 5: Calculating Brand Value
Brands influence consumer choice but their influence differs by market segment.	Based on detailed financial, brand and market knowledge identify and forecast the revenues the brand is expected to generate in the future.	Split the Intangible Earnings into the earnings attributable to the brand and the other intangible assets.	The expected future brand earnings are discounted at a rate that appropriately reflects their risk profile.	Brand value is the NPV of the forecast brand Earnings of each market segment.
The valuation therefore needs to be split into the brands strategically relevant market segments represented by homogeneous non-overlapping customer groups.	From the branded revenues derive Intangible Earnings in the following way:	Identify and quantify the purchase drivers that make consumers buy the branded offer and the specific impact the brand has on these.	Based on an analysis of companies that only operate under one master brand the cost of capital or WACC (weighted average cost of capital) represents the most robust and reliable rate for discounting Brand Earnings.	The NPV calculation comprises the explicit forecast period and the period beyond reflecting the ability of brands to continue generating future cash flow.
Segmentation criteria include product or service offer, consumer attitudes, consumption patterns, distribution channels, geography, existing and new customers, share of wallet, etc.	Branded Revenues -Operating Costs -Applicable Taxes -Charge for Capital employed = Intangible Earnings	Brand Impact is the percentage of customer choice driven by the brand. Brand Earnings are calculated by multiplying the brand Impact percentage with the Intangible Earnings.	The discount rate is used to calculate the Net Present Value (NPV) of the forecast Brand Earnings.	The overall value of the brand is the sum of the segment values.
The valuation is then performed in each of the identified segments.		Brand Earnings represent the earnings only attributable to the brand.		

FIGURE 7.1 Brand valuation methodology

58

on the purchase of semiconductors may result in a higher financial gain. This is crucial information for managing the brand as it impacts positioning, communications, and investments.

It is therefore important to understand the variety of market segments a brand operates in and how deep it has penetrated the different segments. Market segment is defined by two key characteristics. First, the segment needs to be distinguished from other segments according to clear and evident criteria that affect the purchase decisions of consumers in that segment. Second, the behavior and perception pattern of consumers in the segment need to be sufficiently homogenous. Some segmentation approaches are relatively easily defined and deliver clearly distinctive segments. For examples segmentations by industry sector, product, geography, or demographics will provide clearly identifiable groups. Segmentations according to purchase behaviors are less clear-cut but still relatively easily defined by frequency, volume, price, and seasonality. Attitudinal segmentations are in particular important for brands as they refer to perception of needs, relevance, values, image attributes, satisfaction, and recommendation. An attitudinal segmentation is particularly important for brand management purposes as it allows the brand positioning, messaging, and investments to be focused on the most relevant and financially rewarding areas. The key business objective of branding is to influence peoples' minds and attitudes in a way that makes them buy more of a company's product at a higher price again and again. Influencing attitudes leads to desired behaviors and financial outcomes.

Attitudinal segmentations rely, however, on the quality of the survey questions and can differ significantly according to the questions asked. In most cases the segmentation will combine several approaches such as product, geography, consumer behavior, and attitude. The purpose of the segmentation is to identify brand relevant segments for which sufficient marketing and financial data are available. The segments need to be materially and strategically relevant with respect to profitability and actionability. The segmentation will also make the valuation more accurate. However, the approach to segmentation should be commercially pragmatic and fit with the purpose of the valuation. In most cases a valuation for management and controlling purposes will be more detailed as it needs to link specific actions and investments with specific market segments. Accounting valuations are less "granular" as they focus on the overall value of the brand. Once the appropriate segmentation is in place the valuation of the brand is conducted in each of the identified segments. The sum of the segment valuations represents the overall value of the brand.

Step 2: Financial analysis

The brand operates on the "outside" of the business by attracting and securing customer demand. Customer demand converts into purchase price, volume, and frequency. The financial forecast assesses the revenue that the brand is expected to generate in the future. The purpose of a brand valuation is to value the useful life of the brand asset. If the brand and the underlying business are a going concern without any current signs or intentions of folding then the useful life time is considered unlimited. If the useful life of the brand is contractually limited due to a licensing agreement then the forecast has to focus on the time period stipulated in the contractual agreements. If the licensing agreement includes an option of renewal then this can be taken into consideration in the forecast. In most cases the brand is valued as a going concern which means the valuation will cover all future expected cash flows attributable to the brand.

In order to prepare the forecast the first step is to identify historic and current revenues that have been generated by the brand. Then the costs and associated capital required to deliver these revenues needs to be identified. For companies that use only one brand, such as IBM and Samsung, the brand and company's financial information is identical because all company assets support the sale and delivery of the branded offer. For companies that use several brands the financial data need to be identified for each specific brand. In cases where the brand and the underlying operations are clearly separated this information can be obtained at least at cost level. However, in some cases the operations of several brands are so closely intertwined that it is difficult to separate cost and capital employed by brand. In such cases cost and capital employed need to be allocated based on group or consolidated data. Such allocations are ideally based on detailed discussions with management and the finance department. Once the allocation assumptions are identified and agreed brand specific financial data can be obtained. Based on the historical and current financial and brand data a brand specific forecast is prepared. While current and historical analyses provide some guidance the main focus has to be on the expected performance of the brand. Based on a thorough understanding of the macro- and micro-economic conditions in which the brand operates the forecast needs to take into consideration customer needs and behaviors, the brand's positioning in the market place, segment and GDP growth rates, disposable income or budgets, the competitive environment, past and planned brand investments, product innovations, changes in distribution, operating margins, and investment requirements. This is a complex process and requires detailed understanding of the brand and its underlying business. The forecast should capture the demand the brand is expected to generate given the macro-economic outlook. The macro-economic outlook is set by GDP growth rates, inflation rates, and expected consumer spending within the respective category. Within this framework the brand's specific revenue generating capability needs to be assessed according to brand perception and behavioral data. Starting points are historic revenues and the short-term revenue in the budget if available. Volume and value market share as well as pricing and purchase frequency data form the basis for the revenue forecast. Financial forecasting is a combination of art and science embedded in a deep understanding of the brand and its markets. Despite the technical analysis and data input the forecast needs to be assessed according to the soundness not only of the input data but also the overall result. An overly optimistic forecast in sales increases and unrealistic assumptions can render the whole valuation meaningless. It is always important to cross-check the overall result of the revenue forecast with historical performance, competitors, and the market.

The expected demand from the brand is represented by sales price and volume translated into a revenue forecast for the brand. From the forecast revenues all necessary operating costs are subtracted to derive the EBITA. This figure includes the depreciation which is assumed to represent the annual average spend for required capital investments but excludes amortization which represents a return of intangible assets. From the EBITA required taxes and a charge for the capital employed are deducted. Capital employed is the operationally required net fixed assets plus net working capital. The charge for the capital employed represents the adequate return required for the use of the tangible assets necessary to deliver the revenues of the brand. The companies' weighted cost of capital (WACC) is assumed to represent an adequate return on the capital employed as it is the return capital provides (debt and equity) required to provide funds. The WACC concept and calculation is firmly established within the business and finance community and used within most companies. After subtracting taxes and a charge for the capital employed the remaining profit is called intangible earnings as it represents the earnings attributable to the intangible assets. The concept of intangible earnings is similar to economic value added and in particular suitable for valuing bundles of assets with different returns. The result of the financial analysis is a forecast of intangible earnings derived from revenues created by the brand. The forecast is based on a deep understanding of the brand and its market. The forecasts should be based on sound analyses and assumptions. While the past is not guidance for the future, historical analysis should be used to cross-check and verify assumptions. As with all forecasting assumptions these should be transparent, kept as simple as possible, and as complex as necessary. There are good statistical modeling tools available that use a vast array of data to build future scenarios. While these are helpful, they should not be used to build impenetrable black-box models or hide assumptions in overly complex calculations. As most of these models are built on the analysis of the correlations and regressions of historical and current data they tend to predict within existing systems. This can be useful for short-term trends but is very hard to apply for long-term horizons. As most forecast periods stretch between 3 and 10 years there is a need to develop a strategic long-term view – the longer the forecast horizon the higher the margin for error. In most cases the valuation consists of two forecast periods. An explicit and detailed forecast which is, on average, for a 5-year period and a forecast of the cash flow into perpetuity which is mostly the previous year's cash flow multiplied by a long-term growth rate. Although most effort is made in preparing the explicit forecast period the value impact of the perpetuity cash flow is much higher and can easily amount to two-thirds of the overall value. Forecasting is not an exact science as many economic and financial experts experienced in the 2008/9 recession. More data does not automatically translate into more insights and better forecasts. Data modeling and judgment need to feed off each other to deliver the best possible forecast. The forecast needs to represent the best possible view based on the available data and information. The complexity and detail of the forecast will depend on the purpose and the time frame of the valuation. Brand valuations for management purposes will need much more detailed insights and understanding of causal relationships as they are supposed to provide a solid base for the strategic management of the brand. Valuations for financial purposes will focus more on the relative soundness of the financial data.

The financial analysis is a crucial part of brand valuation and needs to be conducted with the same detail and diligence as the marketing analyses. It is important that the financial analysis includes and integrates the available marketing data in order to avoid the financial analysis being conducted separately. The purpose of the financial analysis is to provide a forecast of the intangible earnings.

Step 3: Brand impact

The intangible earnings represent the return of all intangible assets of the branded business. For valuing the brand the brand-specific earnings need to be identified.

That means the intangible earnings need to be split between brand earnings and other intangible earnings. This approach is therefore called the profit-split approach. The brand specific earnings can be identified in different ways. The accounting approach is to assume fictitious returns for the different assets including the brand. These returns are derived from analyzing comparable companies and assets and then deriving a respective return. Such an approach however, relies on the quality of the comparisons made. As mentioned previously in the case of brands comparability is difficult as by definition brands have to be different to create value. The Coca-Cola/Pepsi-Cola comparison makes this evident. In addition such an approach does not identify the brand specific value creating factors. It provides only a number but not a solid economic rationale for the validity of this number. A better and much more suitable approach is to assess how the brand creates revenues relative to the other intangible assets of the business. The brand creates revenues through price, volume, and frequency of purchase. To deliver these branded revenues operating costs and capital are required. They are remunerated according to the cost and capital structure of the underlying business which is reflected in the intangible earnings calculation. However, while the reported financial data provide operating costs, taxes, and capital employed, the WACC and other relevant data do not provide the return of specific intangibles let alone the brand. For that reason the brand-specific earnings need to be separated from the earnings of all intangibles. This approach assesses the brand in its context with other intangibles. By looking at the demand and subsequent revenue generation of the brand its specific contribution to the profit generation of the underlying business can be assessed. The starting point is to identify the way brands create demand and subsequently revenues. This requires analysis and dissection of the purchase decision of customers and consumers. Consumers as well as professional buyers base their purchase decision on a wide range of perceptions and emotions.[1] Modern research techniques can provide a detailed understanding of purchase motives, purchase funnels and how these are impacted by customer perceptions. As discussed in Chapter 1 brands are a combination of promises and experiences that create a certain perception about a company's products and services. As this perception impacts the purchase by customers it represents a good measure for the relative influence the of brand. A customer makes a purchase decision on a variety of criteria. This includes price and availability as well as functional and emotional benefits. The bundle of these purchase drivers leads to a transaction between customers and suppliers. As in nearly all purchase decisions there is a choice between competing products and services. Most brands in the same category will offer similar tangible benefits and a unique mix of intangible benefits. Some of the intangible benefits can also be similar but the overall mix of brand perceptions will be different. For assessing how customers perceive a brand and how this perception then guides their purchase decision appropriate market research data need to be prepared and analyzed. Most companies will have a variety of surveys and research on this subject. The research methodologies can be qualitative and quantitative. Qualitative research has the advantage of probing deeper and being able to provide more detail about brand perception and purchase behavior. Qualitative research comprises of in-depth one-to-one or group interviews as well as focus groups. Through their interactive nature qualitative research can provide unique insights and understanding of brand perceptions and purchase decisions. Observation research is another way of analyzing and understanding shopping behavior through detailed observations and in some cases subsequent interviews. Although qualitative research is most insightful in understanding perceptions and purchase behavior it is limited by the number of interviewees and therefore its statistical relevance. Quantitative research data are required to provide a sufficient number of interviews in order to provide statistically reliable data. Most of the leading market research firms run standardized panel surveys which provide some basic quantitative research.

In addition, most research firms provide tailored surveys to meet specific requirements. Most firms offer surveys that include all main input data such as awareness, relevance, consideration, image attributes, and purchase intention. However, due to their standardization and the increasing use of online surveys the depth of this type of research is limited due to the selection of the questions included in the questionnaire. The quality of the research becomes apparent when purchase drivers and brand perceptions are linked through statistical analyses and modeling. It is not unusual that even tailored and assignment specific research surveys prepared by established market research firms deliver only a limited number of purchase drivers due to overlapping questions and lack of relevant questions. This can impair the result and its usefulness for management. Market research is a topic in its own rights and this book does not intend to provide a comprehensive overview and critique of different market research approaches. It is, however, important to understand the quality of the data input in order to design a suitable model to explain the impact of brands on purchase decisions and value creation. Ideally, the market research is designed specifically to identify and understand the purchase drivers and how they are impacted by the brand. However, due to the relatively high costs of these surveys many companies will want to make use of existing research data. In most cases it is possible to find a way of incorporating the data into a suitable model.

The first step in assessing the impact of the brand on customers' purchase decisions and revenues is to identify the reasons why customers chose to consider and buy a specific brand. There will be functional or tangible and emotional or intangible benefits that drive the purchase. These benefits are at different degrees represented by the brand and its perceptions. Some purchase drivers are entirely dependent on brand perception. They comprise benefits that are based on perception without close comparison or testing of competing offers. These intangible benefits fall into two categories. The first category comprises benefits that are purely emotional and cannot be materially tested and compared. They include perceptions of emotions such as friendliness, approachability, care, status, coolness, stylishness, and happiness (see Figure 7.2).

These perceptions cannot exist without the brand as they are not attached to tangible or testable functionality of the product. Then there are perceptions of functional benefits that can be tested and compared but are mostly assumed in a purchase decision. This is either due to the fact that testing and comparing these benefits is technically difficult and time-consuming or the lack of interest in delving into the detail of

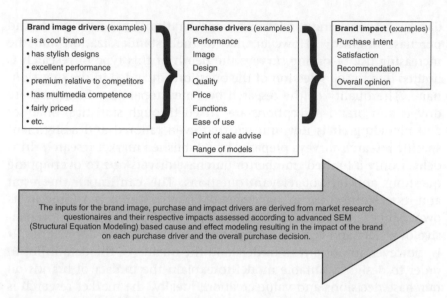

Brand image drivers (examples)	Purchase drivers (examples)	Brand impact (examples)
• is a cool brand	Performance	Purchase intent
• has stylish designs	Image	Satisfaction
• excellent performance	Design	Recommendation
• premium relative to competitors	Quality	Overall opinion
• has multimedia competence	Price	
• fairly priced	Functions	
• etc.	Ease of use	
	Point of sale advise	
	Range of models	

The inputs for the brand image, purchase and impact drivers are derived from market research questionaires and their respective impacts assessed according to advanced SEM (Structural Equation Modeling) based cause and effect modeling resulting in the impact of the brand on each purchase driver and the overall purchase decision.

FIGURE 7.2   **Brand impact assessment (example mobile handset brand) 1**

the offer. For example in the purchase of a TV set consumers will rely on brand perception regarding quality, functionality, reliability, and durability because they will have limited or no means to test and compare these product features. In some cases publicly available test reports will function as a proxy for performing customized comparisons. In many cases a wide range of functional and technical benefits will be included in customers' brand perception. Product quality is a key feature for most products and most brands will include some level of quality perception. The alignment of product features and quality in most categories has made it hard to distinguish products on these levels. In the case of flat panel TVs there are only a small number of suppliers of the screen panels which constitute a major component of the product. As a result, a Sony branded TV will have a screen that is made by a joint venture with Samsung although both brands compete in the same product category. Most consumers will not be aware of this and will regard the brands' product as distinctive and separate offers. Similar examples can be found in the car industry: VW's Touareg and Porsche's Cayenne are built on the same platforms and share most components. Although the Cayenne comes with a more powerful engine option, most reviews could not find significant differences between the two vehicles. Even visually both cars are very similar. The biggest difference is the price as at comparable engine levels the Porsche is about 60 percent more expensive than the VW Touareg. These examples illustrate the fact that many functional and tangible benefits, such as quality, are significantly carried by brand perceptions. Without the brand the quality promise of most products and services would not be credible. The impact of brand perceptions on functional or tangible benefits is very important for B2B brands where emotional benefits can be relevant but not to the same degree as for consumer brands. Professional service brands such as IBM, SAP, PricewaterhouseCoopers, Goldman Sachs, and McKinsey will provide a wide range of functional benefits that are difficult to test and compare. They will offer professional expertise, customer service, efficient project management, and performance improvements which rely strongly on their specific brand perceptions. In some cases, functional benefits can be a brand's main component. The Volvo brand has for decades focused on safety although most comparable cars offered similar safety features and performance. Functional benefits can therefore be very dependent on the brand's perception as the actual differentiation in the delivery and result of the functional benefit is often very similar and hard to distinguish. On the other hand, there are functional benefits that are not dependent on brand perceptions but deliver clear tangible results such as drug or software patents. In the case of professional service firms, specific individuals can have a strong impact on customers' purchase decisions as clients follow them when they leave the firm.

Once the key purchase drivers have been identified they need to be assessed according to their relative importance or impact on customers' purchase decisions. This can be achieved through applying statistical modeling techniques such as structural equation modeling (SEM). Through the statistical analysis process the research results can be translated into single clearly defined purchase drivers. Once the purchase drivers and their relative importance have been assessed, the impact of the brand on the purchase drivers can be determined. From the research the brand perceptions are identified and then assessed according to their impact on the purchase drivers. It is important to analyze the impact of the brand on the purchase driver and not as a separate purchase driver, as the brand represents all perceptions of a company's products and services. As such the brand is closely interwoven with the other tangible and intangible aspects of the offer. In the cases of functional or tangible product drivers it is the combination of brand perception and actual product delivery that drives the purchase. In

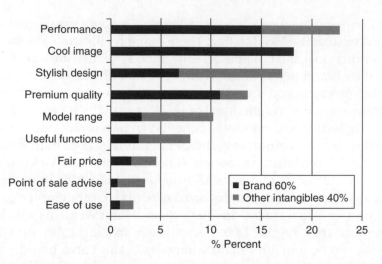

FIGURE 7.3 **Brand impact assessment (example mobile handset brand) 2**

the case of quality and functionality as a purchase driver some aspects can be and are assessed by customers and some not. However, in most situations product quality will be part of brand perception.

Brand impact is measured through a two-tier approach. First, the percentage impact of each purchase driver is assessed (see Figure 7.3). Once the percentage impact of each purchase driver is determined the impact of the brand on each driver is assessed. The result is the brand impact which is the percentage impact brand perceptions have on each of the purchase drivers. These are then multiplied by the percentage impact of the purchase drivers to deriver the overall brand impact. Brand impact varies by driver and brand. The higher the brand impact the higher the dependence of the purchase on the brand. Consumer and luxury goods have an average brand impact of 60–90 percent as most purchase drivers are heavily impacted by brand perception. Coca-Cola, Louis Vuitton, and Nivea are purchased because of the brand perceptions delivered by the underlying product. The Coca-Cola brand's key perceptions are refreshment, American heritage, the original and genuine cola, and fun and enjoyment. Although the brand is supported by a strong global distribution network its success is driven by consumer pull. The Louis Vuitton brand's perception comprises of style, status, luxury, French sophistication, timeless chic, and design. Despite a strong logo display on its core product line up Louis Vuitton has assumed a position of

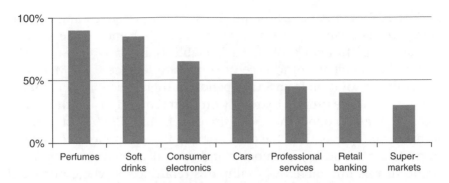

FIGURE 7.4 **Brand impact average by category**

classic and timeless chic. Although the products are of high quality and meticulously manufactured they would lose their customer attraction without the LV brand. Nivea's brand perceptions are wholesomeness, cleanliness, caring as well as credibility, and genuineness built by its long history. The products are well-made but would be indistinguishable without the Nivea brand. Although all these brands have a physical delivery it is the perceptions that consumers have about these brands that drive their purchase. The products are of high quality, within their segments, but the consumer demand for these products is created through emotional brand perceptions. The brand impact is therefore very high and dominates the purchase decision. The underlying product, service and distribution support the creation and maintenance of these brand perceptions. There are categories where the range of the brand impact can be significantly wider (see Figure 7.4). These include consumer durables such as cars and consumer electronics. Here brand impact can vary between 45 and 70 percent.

At the high end are brands such as Apple, Blackberry, BMW, Audi, Porsche, and Mercedes-Benz where despite the equivalent technology involved brand perceptions dominate the purchase. Without Porsche's brand perception the company's cars would still be well-designed, styled, and engineered cars, but customers would lack the prestige, status, and sophistication that these brands represent. In these categories there are also brands where the tangible functional aspects are very important and the brand perception is not about emotional values but represents functional benefits such as quality and durability. Brands in this category include Nissan and Sharp.

Most B2B brands have a brand impact of between 25 and 50 percent. Professional service firms are at the higher end of the scale as the actual performance of the deliverable is hard to measure. The impact on the client of a piece of consulting advice from McKinsey or a software solution from SAP depends on their execution and implementation. These firms live strongly on their reputation and the widely quoted phrase "nobody has been fired for hiring IBM" illustrates the impact brand perceptions have in choosing these suppliers. Low-brand impacts are found in commodity and special industries where non-brand drivers dominate. An example is retail petrol where price and location are the key drivers and the brand impact is below 25 percent. However, in retail lubricants brands can have a very high impact similar to the consumer brands. Brands such as Mobil and Castrol have brand impacts at the high end of the consumer brand range. As noted earlier, brand impact can vary significantly by customer segment, product line, or geography. Toyota and Honda have a higher brand impact in Asia and North America than in Europe where they are predominantly a functional purchase with little or no emotional benefits.

As brand impact measures the relative contribution the brand makes to the overall purchase, it is the most suitable figure to use for determining brand-specific earnings. *Brand earnings* are calculated by multiplying the *intangible earnings* by the *brand impact* percentage. The brand impact analysis provides the most suitable way of assessing brand earnings as it is based on the brand's specific impact on customer purchase decisions and revenue generation.

The brand impact analysis delivers a brand specific contribution to the underlying business. As such it values the brand in a specific and existing context of other intangible and tangible assets. If these circumstances change the brand impact analysis needs to be adjusted accordingly. This would be the case if the brand were taken into a different business context either through sale or extension into new or unrelated areas. For example, in the UK, the Woolworth's brand was sold in June 2009 to a pure online retailer after the operations collapsed and the company had to file for bankruptcy.[2] The new online operations are not yet established but its brand impact will change as there is no store network for brand promotion. That will potentially mean that the brand impact will increase as it will be the Woolworth's brand that will bring customers to the website. It may also make the brand more valuable as it is driving a profitable business model.

The brand impact analysis also provides a key management tool for understanding and managing the brand value creation. Through a detailed understanding of purchase drivers and how they are impacted by brand perceptions, marketing strategies and investments can be optimized according to brand impact. It also provides the impact of each single brand element and the opportunity to design the best fit with the respective customer groups.

Step 4: Discount rate

Once the brand earnings forecast has been completed the appropriate discount rate needs to be determined to calculate the NPV of the brand earnings which represents the value of the brand. According to the Capital Asset Pricing Model (CAPM), the discount rate represents the relationship between risk and expected return. Potential investors need to be compensated in two ways: time value of money and risk. The time value of money is represented by the risk-free rate that compensates for investing money over a period of time. The risk-free rate is best represented by government bond yields. The discount rate needs to reflect the risk of the expected brand earnings relative to the risk-free rate. A high discount rate indicates a high level of risk and therefore a lower expectation that the brand earnings will be delivered as projected. A high discount rate results in a lower NPV. A low discount rate represents a low level of risk and thus a high expectation of achieving these earnings. A low discount rate results in a higher NPV. The discount rate needs to reflect the risk profile of the brand or the likelihood that the brand will deliver the expected earnings. For business valuations according to CAPM the discount rate is represented by a company's weighted cost of capital (WACC). This calculation represents the weighted return to all capital providers according to their contribution in financing the business. The two principal types of capital are debt and equity. The "cost of equity" is the risk-free rate plus the equity risk premium adjusted for the company specific beta. The equity risk premium represents the additional return investors require in order to invest in the more uncertain and therefore riskier return from stocks. The equity risk premium differs according to market, whether it is historical or prospective and whether it is based on arithmetic or geometric averages. However, most practitioners use a premium of between 3.5 percent and 7 percent. The premium is then adjusted for the volatility of a company's stock versus the overall market measured by the beta. The beta of the market is one. A stock that is more volatile than the market has a beta above one. Many technology businesses fall into this category. A stock that is less volatile in its performance versus the stock market has a beta below one. Many consumer staple companies and utilities fall into this category. The cost of debt is the effective rate that a company pays on its debt. Since interest expense is tax deductible, the after-tax rate is most often used. The cost of debt and cost of equity are weighted according to the structure of the capital of the business. The problem with using the WACC for valuing brands is that it is based on the assessment of all business assets combined. The risk of the brand is integrated with that of the other business assets. It is therefore argued by some brand valuation experts that the WACC is too broad for valuing the brand as it does not provide an asset specific risk. In principle this is correct as different assets have different risk profiles. For example, the economic return from R&D assets, such as new patents and technologies, has a much more uncertain outcome than the return from established brands. It is therefore fair to expect that their respective discount rates would differ. This is the reason why many brand specific valuation approaches use an alternative risk assessment that is a hybrid of CAPM and brand specific factor scoring models. As with the CAPM approach the starting point is the risk free rate. To the risk free rate they add a premium that is not driven by the capital structure of the underlying business but by an assessment of the strength of the brand and its market. The brand's risk profile is determined through a set of metrics that look at the brand's competitive position with in its markets and the condition of the markets the brand operates in. These metrics are converted through a distribution curve or logarithm into a brand specific discount rate. The metrics combine macro-economic data, market research data, and assessments of brand management. The data inputs include GDP growth rates, inflation rate, market share, market share growth rates, market ranking, price differentials, customer loyalty, satisfaction and advocacy, consumer perception of brand values, differentiation, relevance, product innovation, marketing spend, advertising effectiveness, consistency of brand communications, and legal IP management. The data are grouped into different assessment topics – some data are selected to be converted into a scoring framework. The alternative brand risk assessment models look at a set of brand metrics that are useful in evaluating the sustainability of the brand's ability to generate future cash flows. As such they are very valuable analyses and can be used within a brand management framework. The alternative brand strength or risk assessment models are however the most challenged elements of many brand valuation methodologies. While CAPM theory and portfolio theory have emerged from decades of corporate finance and practice based on market data dating back to the 1920s, the information and research available on brands is substantially thinner and much patchier. It is therefore difficult to replicate a comparable level of data depth and quality. The other issue with the alternative risk assessment approaches is the actual use and validity of converting a wide range of data into a valid discount rate.

Many approaches have to rely on set of assumptions that have and cannot be verified due to the complex nature of brands. While the profit split to derive brand earnings is based on accepted and tested business concepts and practice it is harder to find a marketing and financial consensus around the alternative discount rate assessment. There are many companies who operate only under one brand or where one brand dominates the company's business such as IBM, Nokia, Starbucks, McDonald's, Apple, BMW, Mercedes-Benz, and HP. The WACC of these companies fairly reflects the risk of their brands in their current use because the risks of all assets are intertwined. The analysis of companies operating under a master brand suggests that there is little evidence for a meaningful split between brand and business discount rate. It is therefore more robust and reliable to use the WACC for discounting brand earnings.

Determining a suitable discount rate is often the most difficult and uncertain part of a DCF valuation. This is made worse by the fact that the NPV is very sensitive to the choice of discount rate as a small change in the discount rate causes a large change in the overall value.

In the end the discount rate needs to be credible to a financial audience. The theory for a pure brand-specific discount rate independent of the CAPM framework is interesting but not practical and with the current data availability difficult to implement. This is demonstrated by companies that operate under only one "master brand." It is therefore advisable to use the WACC as a brand discount rate in situations where the brand is used in all or the main cash flow generating activities of the business. In cases where the brand is part of a large portfolio and does not represent the majority of the business, the WACC should be adjusted according to a range of betas available for the respective industry. The discount rate is used to calculate the net present value (NPV) of the expected future brand earnings.

Step 5: Calculating brand value

The value of the brand is the sum of the NPVs of the forecast brand earnings of the identified segments in which the brand is valued. The value consists of two sets of discounted brand earnings. The first set is the detailed forecast as discussed in the previous section. The detailed forecast normally covers a period of five years, though longer time-frames are also used. If a brand is valued as an on-going concern its value creation will extend beyond the explicit forecast period. The second set is the terminal value which represents the brand earnings beyond the explicit forecast into perpetuity. The brand earning of the last year of the explicit forecast period from the basis for the terminal value calculation. A constant growth rate (e.g. long-term nominal GDP growth rate) is used to grow these brand earnings into perpetuity. The long-term growth rate needs to represent the growth potential of the brand's earnings into perpetuity. The selection of the brand earnings forecast for the terminal value calculation is very important as in many valuations the terminal value exceeds the NPV of the explicit forecast. For that reason the brand earnings number used for the terminal value should reflect the long-term ability of the brand to generate these cash flows. This is the reason why in some cases the earnings figure for the terminal value calculation is adjusted. The terminal brand value is then calculated by dividing the final brand's earnings beyond the forecast period by the discount rate minus the long-term growth rate. The brand value is then the sum of the NPV of the explicit forecast and the terminal value. The valuation is different for situations in which the time for the use of the brand is limited. This would be the case for a licensing agreement with an agreed time limit. Under such circumstances brand earnings are forecast only for the period of the licensing agreement. An exemplary brand value calculation for a fictitious mobile handset brand is shown in Table 7.1.

The outlined valuation approach aligns the value of brands with established and widely used valuation approaches. Through brand valuation brands become comparable to other business assets as well as the overall company value.

CONCLUSION

It is important to bear in mind that a valuation approach delivers a framework but not an automated answer. Brand valuation is a derivative of business valuation and therefore, faces similar issues. In the debate about valuing brands the precision or lack of precision is still a major point of discussion. There are different approaches and views on what is the right or correct way of valuing brands. The five-step model outlined a framework that provides the most robust and reliable results. However, the model is only one part of the equation. A fair and robust valuation requires the right data inputs and assumptions. As with a DCF model or other valuation approaches the same model does not provide the same value. All valuation frameworks and in particular the ones that are based on forecasts carry a significant level of uncertainty. In spite of the availability of a wide range of marketing and financial data a valuation is always at a point in time, and as such subject to change.

As outlined in Chapter 2 the valuation of brands is a complex affair as it requires a detailed understanding of marketing and finance. The question that arises is: Why bother with all the complications of valuing brands? The answer is relatively simple. With the established understanding that brands are key corporate assets the need has emerged for the economic valuation of brands for a wide range of management and transaction requirements. The following chapters will deal in detail with the diverse use of brand valuation in management, commerce, and finance.

TABLE 7.1 Brand valuation of mobile handset brand

		Year 1	Year 2	Year 3	Year 4	Year 5
Market (units)		1,059,755,749	1,232,495,936	1,461,740,180	1,626,916,821	1,727,785,663
Market growth rate (%)			16.3	18.6	11.3	6.2
Market share (volume) (%)		12.3	14.2	17.6	16.1	16.8
Volume		130,349,957	175,014,423	257,266,272	261,933,608	290,267,991
Price per unit (US$)		26.0	29	30	26	24
Price change (%)			10.0	6.0	−15.0	−5.0
Branded revenues		3,389,098,885	5,005,412,496	7,799,284,293	6,749,662,374	7,105,809,776
Cost of goods sold		1,355,639,554	1,751,894,373	2,729,749,503	2,362,381,831	2,487,033,422
Gross margin		2,033,459,331	3,253,518,122	5,069,534,791	4,387,280,543	4,618,776,355
Marketing costs		847,274,721	1,351,461,374	2,027,813,916	1,687,415,593	1,776,452,444
Depreciation		149,120,351	220,238,150	274,534,807	267,286,630	281,390,067
Other overheads		542,255,822	800,865,999	1,637,849,702	1,214,939,227	1,207,987,662
EBITA (Earnings before interest, tax, and amortization)		494,808,437	880,952,599	1,129,336,366	1,217,639,092	1,352,946,181
Applicable taxes	35.0%	173,182,953	308,333,410	395,267,728	426,173,682	473,531,164

NOPAT (net operating profit after tax)		321,625,484	572,619,190	734,068,638	791,465,410	879,415,018
Capital employed		2,135,132,298	3,153,409,872	4,913,549,105	4,252,287,296	4,476,660,159
Working capital		643,928,788	951,028,374	1,481,864,016	1,282,435,851	1,350,103,858
Net PPE		1,491,203,510	2,202,381,498	3,431,685,089	2,969,851,445	3,126,556,302
Capital charge	8.3%	177,215,981	261,733,019	407,824,576	352,939,846	371,562,793
Intangible earnings		144,409,504	310,886,170	326,244,062	438,525,564	507,852,225
Brand impact	60.0%					
Brand earnings		86,645,702	186,531,702	195,746,437	263,115,339	304,711,335
Discount rate (WACC)	8.3%					
Discount brand earnings		80,005,265	159,036,108	154,102,078	191,263,606	204,524,965
NPV of discounted brand earnings (years 1–5)		788,932,023				
Long-term growth rate	2.5%					
NPV of terminal value (beyond Year 5)		3,337,442,113				
Brand value		4,126,374,136				

CHAPTER 8

BRANDS ON THE BALANCE SHEET

The debate about the value of brands became the driver for the recognition of intangible assets on balance sheets around the world. In 1988, Rank Hovis McDougall (RHM), a leading British food group listed on the London stock exchange, recorded its non-acquired brands as intangible assets on its balance sheet in a defense against a hostile bid by Australian takeover specialist Goodman Fielder Wattie (GFW). The bid came at a time when value focused investment vehicles exploited the value gap created by the relatively low market values of many companies with strong brands. For example, in 1986 the Hanson Trust had acquired Imperial Group for UK£2.3 billion. It then sold the group's undervalued food portfolio for UK£2.1 billion and retained a highly cash generative tobacco business which net acquisition costs were just about UK£200 million for a business that generated an operating profit of UK£74 million.[1]

At the time accountants and equity analysts were substantially undervaluing companies with valuable brand assets. RHM therefore decided as part of its defense against the GFW bid to have its brand portfolio valued and included on its balance sheet. The results were quite remarkable. While RHM's tangible assets amounted to about UK£400 million the brand portfolio was valued at UK£678 million. Based on the value of the brand investors reassessed the value of RHM which led to a significant increase in its share price which soured the deal for GFW and prompted a withdrawal of the bid. In the same year RHM was fighting off GFW's takeover bid, the UK drinks conglomerate Grand Metropolitan, which later merged with Guinness to become what is today Diageo, reported the value of its acquired brands on its balance sheet. Quite clearly brand-owning companies felt the need to deal with their intangible assets on their balance sheets. The accounting treatment of intangibles assets revealed that accounting standards had neglected the main wealth creating assets in companies and that their regulations could disadvantage companies purchasing businesses with strong brands or other intangibles. Accounting rules had focused predominantly on tangible assets as they could be easily assessed on a cost base and expected to have value in case of a liquidation of the business. This followed the tradition that value creation was mainly a result of the efficient purchase and use of land and manufacturing facilities. This was reflected in the stock markets by relatively low price to book values. However, the financial transactions of the 1980s and rising price to book values of many companies indicated that intangible assets became increasingly important for corporate value. As a result, acquisition prices of companies included an increasingly significant premium over the net assets of the acquired business. The result was what the accountants called goodwill. Goodwill was the catch-all for intangible assets and wealth creating items that were hard to value and negligible relative to the tangible assets. As long as the differences between acquisition prices and net assets were small, goodwill was a minor accounting issue. However, as the goodwill on acquisition increased the issue of dealing with this ever increasing accounting item became important to management and financial markets.

At the time, accounting standards in most markets including the US and Europe required companies to write-off goodwill from acquisitions against reserves. As a result a company could, through the acquisition of a business with valuable brands or other intangible assets for which it had to pay a significant premium over and above net assets, end up with significantly reduced equity as it has to write-off the goodwill against reserves. Clearly, accounting standards were out of sync with business reality.

Initially, accounting bodies were strongly opposed to recognizing intangible assets on the balance sheet. Only in Australia and New Zealand did accounting regulations allow capitalizing intangible assets (acquired and internally generated) on the balance sheet. Prominent companies in these markets made use of this opportunity. Lion Nathan (a leading beer and drinks group in the region), Fontera (a leading dairy conglomerate), and Telecom NZ capitalized their internally generated brands on the balance sheet. For example, in Lion Nathan's September 2005 financial statements brands accounted for NZ$2.4 billion of the total assets of NZ$4.1 billion which was more than half of the company's reported asset base. Fonterra, reported intangibles of NZ$1.47 billion, including goodwill of NZ$220 million and purchased brands of NZ$1.2 billion. Telecom NZ published the value of its brand assets in the supplementary information of its 1998 financial statements. In that year, brands constituted 36 percent of the total assets and 14.6 percent of Telecom's enterprise value. Although these were exceptions they demonstrated that brands accounted for a substantial part of corporate wealth and they could be reliably valued, independently audited, and recognized on companies balance sheets.[2]

It was, however, the valuation of brands and their inclusion in the balance sheet of RHM and other brand-owning companies in the UK that triggered the accounting debate on the treatment of intangible assets. It took nearly a decade for accounting bodies around the world to adjust to the new business paradigm. In 1997, the UK Standards Board was the first to react by issuing FRS (Financial Reporting Standard) 10 and 11 on the treatment of acquired goodwill on the balance sheet. A year later, the International Accounting Board followed suit with IAS (International Accounting Standard) 38 superseding the UK standards. In 2001 the US Accounting Standards Board introduced FAS (Federal Accounting Standard) 141 and 142 abandoning the pooling of accounting and laying out detailed rules on the treatment of acquired goodwill on the balance sheet. Today most companies follow either the rules of the IAS or ASB. Although the IAS and the FAS are similar in most aspects when dealing with intangible assets including brands there are two significant differences.[3] They clearly differentiate between internally generated and acquired intangible assets. As a result acquired brands appear on the balance sheet but internally generated brands do not. So the Burger King brand appears on the accounts of Burger King Holdings because it was acquired while the McDonald's brand does not appear on the company's balance sheet as it was internally generated.

The recognition of intangible assets happens within the overall allocation of the purchase price to all of the acquired assets and liabilities in proportion to their fair value. This is known as the Purchase Price Allocation (PPA). This requires the different assets to be identified and valued. The standards have defined intangible assets according to several categories. These are described in Table 8.1.

From an accounting view the marketing related intangible asset represent the brand. As the definitions are driven by legal title and separability the list does not necessarily fit with the more holistic marketing and management view of brands. However, for accounting purposes the brand is sufficiently represented by the marketing related intangible assets. In practice, the marketing related intangibles are rarely separately valued and mostly bundled and valued as brand assets because a meaningful separation and valuation is in most cases neither possible

TABLE 8.1 Intangible asset categories

Intangible asset categorization according to IFRS 3

Marketing	Customer	Artistic	Technology	Contracts
• Trademarks, trade names • Service marks, collective marks, certification marks • Trade dress (unique color, shape, or package design) • Newspaper mastheads • Internet domain names • Non-competition agreements	• Customer lists • Order or production backlog • Customer contracts and related customer relationships • Non-contractual customer relationships	• Plays, operas, ballets • Books, magazines, newspapers, other literary works • Musical works such as compositions, song lyrics, and advertising jingles • Pictures, photographs • Video and audiovisual material, including motion pictures, music videos, television	• Patented technology • Computer software and mask works • Unpatented technology • Databases, including title plants • Trade secrets, such as secret formulas, processes, recipes	• Licensing, royalty, standstill agreements • Advertising, construction, management, service • Lease agreements • Construction permits • Franchise agreements • Operating and broadcast rights • Use rights such as drilling, water, air, mineral, timber cutting, and route authorities • Servicing contracts such as mortgage servicing contracts • Employment contracts

nor practical. Once the assets are defined their fair value is assessed according to valuation methods prescribed by the standards. Various valuation approaches, each of them based on several different methods, can be employed.

While the fair value of the assets and liabilities already reported in the balance sheet of the acquired business is relatively easy, the valuation of intangible assets such as brands, patents, customer relations, or technologies is more difficult as no recorded and audited value exists. The identified intangible assets need to be valued according to the fair value approach. Fair value is defined as the amount at which an asset could be exchanged between knowledgeable willing parties in an arm's length transaction. With intangible assets accounting for about three-quarters of corporate wealth, they tend to constitute the central value drivers of the acquired company and are, therefore, most important to the acquiring company in the acquisition process. The fair value of these intangible assets must then be determined in accordance with prescribed valuation approaches and methods.

The favored approach is the market approach where the fair value represents the value of a comparable asset in an active market. Alternatively, the price of a comparable market transaction can be used, subject to comparability criteria regarding the similarity between the two intangible assets. The key problem of this approach is the fact that for most intangible assets an active market does not exist and comparable market transactions are scarcely available, if at all. This is a particular issue for brands as they are rarely sold without an underlying business and the number of such transactions is very small. Most brands are sold in the context of an active business. Second, the unique nature of brands makes any comparable approach problematic as discussed in Chapter 5.

The secondary, but in practice most often employed valuation approach, is the income approach. The value of the intangible asset is determined by discounting the future cash flows expected to accrue during the estimated remaining economic useful life. There are two types of income approaches. The first is called the multi-period excess earnings method which values an intangible asset in the context of other tangible or intangible assets. By subtracting fictitious payments for the supporting assets the remaining "excess" cash flows are attributed to the asset to be valued. The second income approach is the incremental cash flow method where the cash flows of the acquired company with the relevant intangible asset are compared to a fictitious company without this asset. The difference represents the "incremental" cash flow attributed to the intangible asset. In both cases the cash flows are discounted to their NPV. Both approaches are problematic. The multi-period approach relies on the quality and reliability of the charges for the supporting assets which is difficult to obtain and prone to questionable assumptions. The incremental cash flow approach, as discussed in Chapter 5, is not suitable for valuing brands as there are almost no unbranded offers available against which the brand could be compared.

Due to the difficulties involved in the market and income approaches most accounting firms use the relief from royalty method for valuing brands. It is based on the assumption that an external third party would be prepared to pay a license fee for the use of a brand or a patent that it does not own. The value of the intangible asset is then calculated as the NPV of the unpaid license fee. The validity of this approach is based on the assumption that reliable comparable royalty payments for brands can be obtained. However, as the example of the Coca-Cola and Pepsi-Cola brands demonstrates, even brands that are so similar with respect to product, target group, distribution, and price can vary significantly in value. While comparability may work for some of the other intangible assets listed is certainly fails to capture the fair value of brands. In addition, using reported royalty rates is very problematic as these differ by use and markets. Additionally, in many cases there are hidden costs or conditions which are not disclosed but affect the economic benefit generated by the brand license.[4]

The most suitable approach to valuing brands values the brand according to its assets specific value creation (see Chapter 7). It is interesting to note that the accounting profession has also recognized the limitations of the other valuation approaches. In 2007, the International Standards Valuation Committee (ISVC) published a discussion paper on determining the fair value of intangible assets for IFRS reporting, providing a more detailed approach to intangible assets and their valuations. They suggest different valuation approaches depending on the comparability of these assets. The ISVC recognizes that some intangible assets such as brands are so unique in their nature that they cannot be valued by comparison but only according to the specific cash flow they can produce. This is in line with the valuation approach framework detailed in this book.

Once the intangible assets have been identified and valued they are capitalized according to their fair value. The difference between purchase price of the acquired business and the sum of the fair values of the acquired assets and liabilities is capitalized as goodwill. The capitalized values are subject to annual impairment tests. The purpose of the impairment test is to assess whether the asset value is still fair or needs to be adjusted. Intangible assets with a definite (limited) life are amortized according to their remaining economic useful life on a scheduled basis mostly at the same annual amount. Intangible assets with an indefinite life are also subject to a regular impairment test, and are thus exposed to the risk of unscheduled impairment charges. According to IAS 38, intangible assets have an indefinite life when "there is no foreseeable limit to the period over which the asset is expected to generate net cash flows for the entity."[5] Brands qualify in most cases as intangible assets with an indefinite life. This is fair as many brands have demonstrated an astonishing durability. Of the leading 100 brands covered in the annual *BusinessWeek* survey about 70 percent have been in existence for more than 50 years. The value of the intangible asset is adjusted according to the impairment test. If the value is higher or the same no impairment has occurred and the asset value on the balance sheet remains unchanged. The value cannot increase. If however, the impairment value is lower the balance sheet value of the asset needs to be reduced and the impaired value amount is expensed through the income statement. Despite these elaborate valuation rules the actual detail of the reporting on intangible assets tends to be rather thin. Even companies such as The Coca-Cola Company or P&G that are mainly brand driven disclose very little about their acquired brands compared to their tangible assets and other investments. Although the values of intangible assets and goodwill are reported there is little or no detail as to which specific brands and assets they refer. Overall, the reporting detail on tangible and financial assets by far outstrips the reporting on acquired intangible assets.

The debate about brands on the balance sheet has had a significant impact on the treatment of intangible assets on the balance sheet. However, the resultant changes in the accounting standards have been more a pragmatic solution for the accountants to deal with the increasing goodwill in acquisitions than an alignment of the balance sheet with commercial reality. The accounting rules on acquired goodwill are a half-way house in their dealings with brands as well as with other intangible assets. They only recognize those brand assets that have been subject of an acquisition. As a result, internally generated intangible assets are still not recognized. While this may be convenient and understandable from a technical accounting point of view, it is clearly at odds with economic reality.

The new standards have also blurred the valuation principles of the balance sheet. By putting values on the balance sheet that are based on the expected future cash flows, accounting standards have changed the nature of the balance sheet which used to be a costs-based record of historical investment. While the acquisition price is the cost a company paid for the purchase of another business it is based on a NPV of future expected earnings. Splitting up the value of intangible assets such as brands according to this principle means putting DCF-based fair values next to pure asset cost values such as land, buildings, and machinery.

The question then arises: Why are the acquired assets fairly valued and the internally generated not? From an accounting aspect, the answer is relatively simple. For the acquired intangible assets a transaction-based cost value provides a fair market value. For internally generated assets this is not the case. While this helps to balance the books it is unsatisfactory from an economic value perspective as the majority of corporate value is not accounted for on the balance sheet. The original idea of the balance sheet was to record the cost of assets the firm uses to generate revenues and profits. It also provided a basis for the liquidation value of the business. For the majority of businesses this is now of little use as the business value is mainly generated by intangible assets not accounted for on the balance sheet. The same is true for analysts and investors. Changes in the accounting regime that are not cash flow effective have little impact on investors' and analysts' views on companies' share prices.

Intangible assets account for the majority of business value as evidenced by an average price to tangible book value of the S&P 500 over the past 25 years of 3.9. Brands are among the most important intangible assets accounting, on average, for about one-third of shareholder value. In many leading companies, brands are the single most important and valuable asset. As such the new accounting standards exacerbate the conceptual problem with the current logic of the balance sheet. It is supposed to represent the fair value of a company's assets but fails to account sufficiently for the majority corporate value.

Due to the permanent revaluation of share prices there will always be a difference between book and market value. The question about the best approach to fill this gap in order to align financial reporting with economic reality remains. The current balance sheet treatment of brands and other intangibles provides very little information on these assets. Goodwill and intangible assets have now a clear place on the balance sheet but there is little information beyond the actual figures. If the balance sheet is supposed to give capital providers an insight about the brand as an economic asset then the reporting is doing a rather poor job. There is also an issue with the depth and quality of the valuations. In particular for brands the most widely used approach is the royalty relief method which relies on the quality of comparable royalty rates. While this may be suitable for some intangible assets it is certainly not for brands which by their very nature are different. Another issue is the fact that the purchase price allocation easily becomes a regulatory required administrative task rather than a source of valuable information for investors. The majority of brand valuations conducted by accounting firms are performed in a bundled valuation of all intangible assets with a focus on the allocation issue.

The fact that companies with high brand values have significantly higher price to book ratios than companies with little or no brand value provides clear evidence of the systematic under-reporting of assets.[6] Consequently, the balance sheets of companies with high brand values are unlikely to represent their asset base due to the omission of some measure of brand value. Accounting standards may need to consider including reliable measures of intangible assets, like brand value, to enhance the representational integrity of balance sheets. The current regulations are insufficient in that respect. Due to the important nature of brands there needs to be reflection of their value creation based on a suitable asset specific valuation approach. This does not have to be the balance sheet but an additional form of reporting that provides sufficient information on the value and health of companies' brands and other intangible assets could be suitable. This will not explain the value gap between balance sheet and market value but will improve the disclosure of one of the single most important and valuable business assets.

CHAPTER 9

BRAND SECURITIZATION

The asset value of brands is increasingly used to raise debt financing for a wide range of financial transactions. A key tool for this purpose is securitization. This is a structured financial process that involves the repackaging of cash-flow-producing assets into securities, which are then sold to investors. The securitization of intangible assets such as brands has evolved into an established corporate financing tool used to facilitate M&A, stock buy-backs, and risk transference to investors. As companies recognized that intangibles assets constituted a main portion of their corporate wealth their desire to use them like their tangible assets for financing increased. Chapter 2 established that about two-thirds of business value can be attributed to intangible assets. The total asset value of global intellectual property is estimated to be between US$4 trillion and US$7 trillion. In 2008, intellectual property (IP) licensing revenue worldwide exceeded US$500 billion (compared with an estimated US$18 billion for 1990). For example, IBM alone receives between US$1.5 billion and US$2 billion in annual licensing revenue. In addition, due to new worldwide accounting standards on the treatment of intangible assets their visibility has increased significantly.[1]

A company can use securitization to raise finance by transferring the interests in identifiable cash flows to investors either with or without the support of further collateral. The transferred assets need to generate regular and predictable cash flows which form the basis of the securitization loan or the asset-backed security (ABS). In a typical transaction, the company sells its rights in the cash flow-generating asset(s) to a special purpose vehicle (SPV) company in return for a lump-sum payment. The SPV funds the purchase of these assets by issuing the ABS debt to investors which is repaid with the cash flows generated by the asset(s). Securitization offers a range of financial advantages. The obvious one is immediate cash. In addition, securitization offers a better credit rating and thus cheaper financing costs and a broader class of investors.

Traditionally, the typical asset class in ABS transactions was derived from tangible assets such as real estate, mortgage portfolios, and aircraft leases. However, with the increased awareness and understanding of the importance of the value creation of intangible assets investors' interest in intellectual property (IP) backed securities has risen significantly. The most active IP classes for securitization have been film receivables, franchise fees, brands licensing, and patent licensing royalties. Brands have been subject to some of the largest IP securitization transactions. Most of these transactions have been assessed by the established rating agencies such as Moody's and S&P. Due to the economic nature of brands and the reliability of their cash flows the majority of transactions have received high investment grade ratings from AAA to Ba3.

The term "intellectual property" refers to a set of legal rights that rest with the creators of original concepts, brands, products, and inventions and allow them to prevent others from using it. IP rights that lend themselves to securitization are patents, copyrights, and trademarks. Brands can be protected by several sets of IP rights, most notably trademarks and copyrights. Established brands are particularly attractive to ABS investors as they meet the key securitization criteria of being proven, steady, and predictable. The acceptance of brands in ABS transactions has been helped by the increased acceptance of brand valuation techniques by the financial community. Many prominent brands have been subjects of securitizations. In 1993, the securitization of the Calvin Klein brand for future sales of its perfume products generated a US$58 million loan. GUESS? raised US$75 million through securitizing its domestic and international trademark licenses for watches, shoes, handbags, clothing, and eyewear to repay parts of their debts. Each GUESS? trademark license agreement requires the licensee to pay the higher of a minimum payment or a percentage of sales (between 6–10 percent), with expected royalties of between US$23 and US$22 million for the first few years of issue, before declining when the licenses expired. Standard & Poor rated the deal a BBB. JP Morgan Securities underwrote the securitization with a maturity date of June 2011.[2]

In 2003, UCC Capital completed the first securitization of franchise revenues from Athlete's Foot for a "brand portal" concept based on the revenues from the franchisees, who had to pay an upfront fee of US$35,000 and 5 percent of on-going royalties. The bond raised an estimated US$30–$50 million. Moody's rated the deal Baa3. The deal survived the bankruptcy of the parent company, Athlete's Foot

Brand Inc, in December 2004, demonstrating the level of security brand-backed cash flows could provide.

Brands have been the source of some of the largest IP securitizations.[3] In the UK, one of the largest private equity deals was financed through securitizing a brand portfolio. In 2000 Tomkins PLC a diversified conglomerate agreed to sell the British food business Rand Hovis McDougal (RHM) to Doughty Hanson, a private equity fund, for UK£1.1 billion in a highly leveraged deal. At the time RHM was carrying assets on the balance sheet totaling just UK£300 million. However, Doughty Hanson required an amount of UK£650 million to pay off a bank loan that it had taken out to acquire RHM. RHM's CFO Michael Schurch and his financial advisors decided to structure a financing facility by transferring all of RHM's brands into separate intellectual property companies which were then licensed back to the operating divisions. The transaction was backed by a detailed valuation of RHM's brand portfolio which was also included in the offer document. This securitization became famous as the "Brand Bond" as it was backed by five of the company's oldest brands with the most reliable cash flows, including Hovis bread and Bisto gravy. The bond was structured in several tranches of investment-grade and junk bonds raising a total amount of UK£650 million. This was the largest sterling corporate bond issue at the time. The UK£650 million was used to repay bank loans, and annual financing costs dropped from UK£93 million to UK£80 million.[4]

Over the past few years the size of brand-backed securitizations has increased dramatically. An example is the securitization of the franchise fees by the Dunkin' Donuts, Baskin Robbins, and Togo's brands. This was the first securitization of franchise rights to be used as financing for a corporate takeover. Dunkin' Brands (Dunkin' Donuts, Baskin-Robbins and Togo's) raised US$1.7 billion by securitizing assets of its franchises in fast food chains in a triple-A rated offer. The funds were used for the financing of the US$2.4 billion acquisition of Dunkin' Brands by a consortium of three private equity firms: the Carlyle Group; Thomas H. Lee Partners; and Bain Capital.[5]

In 2006, Sears & Kmart Holdings Inc. raised US$1.8 billion through a securitization of the Kenmore, Craftsman, and DieHard brands. The company transferred ownership of the brands to another entity called KCD IP (Kenmore Craftsman DieHard Intellectual Property). KCD IP charges Sears royalty fees for the use of those brands with which it pays the interest on the issued bonds. Sears has sold the bonds to its insurance subsidiary, where, they serve as protection against potential future loss. The insurance protects Sears from potential financial trouble at a lower cost than Sears could have obtained from an outside party. The KCD IP bonds have a higher credit rating than Sears' regular bonds. Moody's Investors Service has given KCD IP an investment-grade rating of Baa2, four grades better than Sears' junk rating of Ba1. This transaction is notable for being more than 20 times larger than the next largest trademark licensing deal, indicating that strong brands with long performance histories can support large levels of debt at investment grade ratings. It was also the first completed trademark securitization that did not include an apparel brand.[6]

These large brand-backed securitization deals have prompted claims that the potential for a market in bonds backed by intangible assets could become larger than the market for junk bonds. Some companies have started building a whole business model around the securitization of brands. For example, after acquiring the Athlete's Foot chain, Bill Blass apparel brand, and the Maggie Moo's and Marble Slab Creamery ice-cream stores NexCen Brands Inc. has created an entity to hold the brands and issue bonds backed by franchising fees from the sneaker and ice-cream chains, and from Bill Blass licensing fees. The diversity of those fees will enable NexCen to issue lower-cost bonds to pay off earlier debts and fund further acquisitions.[7]

With intangible assets accounting for more than two-thirds of shareholder value and brands accounting for the majority of this amount it is likely that brand-backed securitizations will increase in size and number. These transactions are also a strong indication for recognition of brands as cash-flow generating assets.

CHAPTER 10

BRAND VALUE IN MERGERS AND ACQUISITIONS

Due to their substantial contribution to shareholder value brands have a significant role in most M&A transactions. In the attempt to maximize the proceeds from such transactions buyers and sellers will look at the value of brand assets to see whether it can benefit their position. Depending on the subject of the transaction this can include an asset specific valuation. There are four key areas in which a brand value assessment can benefit an M&A transaction. First, when a business is mainly driven by a brand then the brand value assessment will provide the core of the business valuation. Second, when only the brand is the subject of a transaction without an underlying business then brand valuation is the only way to assess the transaction value. Third, if the transaction is a merger in which two businesses are expected to be united under one brand then it needs to be assessed which brand would add more value to the combined business. Finally, the acquired brands will need to be valued for inclusion on the balance sheet.

If the brand and the underlying business are closely intertwined, brand and business valuation will often go hand in hand as the business will be sold or purchased as an integrated operating unit rather than a bundle of single assets. This is the case for the sale and purchase of branded businesses such as Gillette. In such cases, the main benefit from understanding the value of the brand is its function in generating the business cash flows rather than separating the brand's cash flow from the rest of the operations. The brand valuation framework provides a solid basis for assessing a business value as it is built on integrating marketing and financial analyses. This is due to the fact that brand value looks at the consumer or customer of the brand as the key source of value. The brand valuation framework can be used to assess the additional value the brand can generate in new markets or applications. It can also help in assessing cost synergies and marketing support as well as manufacturing and distribution thresholds, e.g., identifying the level at which cost savings are hurting brand perceptions and affecting consumers' purchase decisions. Prada, Gucci, LVMH, Swatch Group, L'Oréal, P&G, and Unilever have been prime buyers and sellers of branded businesses. Personal experience has shown that in numerous M&A transactions the brand value perspective could add substantial value by increasing the final sales price by up to 40 percent. For example, in the case of a prominent premium beer brand the brand valuation assessment generated a significantly better perspective on the value potential of the brand in export markets which were the key source of future value. The conventional business valuation performed by investment bankers and management consultants did not deliver such insights. In another situation a fashion label was acquiring several designer brands to benefit from marketing, manufacturing, and distribution synergies. While there were significant cost savings in media buying, raw material procurement and distribution, the brand value assessment could identify and quantify the synergy limits with respect to design and production in order to keep and enhance the value of the acquired brands. The brand value assessment is also very important in situations where the business that is bought or sold is a loss-making business. When Tata Motors acquired Jaguar and Land Rover from Ford it did not buy a profitable operation with a solid cash flow but it purchased two brands with significant customer attraction as well as technology and manufacturing expertise. Jaguar had been making a loss for more than a decade but the brand had the potential to deliver positive cash flows in the future. The brand potential of Jaguar was one of the most important assets in this transaction. Other good examples in this respect have been the acquisitions of the Bentley and Rolls-Royce marks by VW and BMW respectively. Although there was a bizarre twist when VW bought Rolls-Royce Motors without owning the Rolls-Royce brand both companies completely revamped the model line. Through infusing their design and operational expertise into the brands they were able to convert two loss-making marks into leading luxury car brands. However, without the brand this would have been impossible. The Bentley and Rolls-Royce examples demonstrate how important these brands have been for the current success of the businesses. Daimler's revitalization of the Maibach brand has been much less successful, not least because it does not have the brand attraction of the other two marks.[1]

Pure brand transactions where only the trademark and related brand titles are sold are relatively rare occasions and tend to be relativaly small transactions. Famous trademarks are only sold if the underlying operations have failed or the business went into liquidation. One of the most famous cases was BMW's acquisition of the rights to the Rolls-Royce brand for UK£40 million in 1998. The deal was the result of complex negotiation between BMW, VW, and Rolls-Royce plc the aircraft engine manufacturer after VW had acquired Rolls-Royce Motor Cars Ltd. the maker of Bentley and Rolls-Royce motor cars. VW had not realized that the right to the Rolls-Royce trademark did not belong to the car business but to the aircraft-engine maker.[2] It became a textbook case on trademark due diligence in M&A transactions. The sale of the Woolworth's brand in the UK is a more recent exaple of a pure brand sale. After the business went into receivership its assets were sold separately. The brand was purchased in March 2009 by the Close Brothers a private equity group that wants to use the brand purely for Internet retailing.[3]

The value of brands can also have significant impact on M&A involving the corporate brands. In many mergers and takeovers the question arises as to which corporate brand should be used for the merged company. Assessing the value of the brands involved helps to make the most economically beneficial decision. Even if one of the companies is the stronger party in the merger, or the merger is in fact a disguised takeover, the decision on the brand for the combined entity requires careful consideration. One of the most prominent examples has been the acquisition of AT&T by SBC Communications then one of the leading regional telecoms in the US. In its markets SBC was well regarded by consumers and corporate customers. The AT&T brand on the other hand, had, despite its 120 year history, been tarnished by poor customer service and many years of mismanagement. After careful brand analyses and evaluation, SBC's CEO Edward E. Whitacre Jr. announced that the new company would adopt the AT&T brand due to its heritage and international reputation. This came as a surprise to many marketing experts.[4] The AT&T brand was capitalized at US$4.9 billion accounting for 31 percent of the acquisition price of US$16 billion.[5] Given that a significant portion of the purchase price was attributable to the AT&T brand, adopting the brand for the combined operation was a good use of investors' funds. Otherwise, an asset with a value of several billion dollars would have to be written off.

According to different research studies, the majority of mergers fail in the integration and implementation process. In the case of corporate brands it is important to understand the wider implication for all key stakeholders. While customers are the most important stakeholders, as they buy the company's products or services, employees can also be crucial particularly in the service sector where they directly deliver the brand in interactions with the customers. Companies can develop very strong corporate cultures of which the brand is the most visible expression. In choosing the brand for a merged operation, employee sentiment needs to be carefully considered. For example, a first-hand consultation with a leading global financial services institution on a potential re-branding of some large subsidiaries showed different responses to the re-branding. While it was possible from the customers' perspective, who had no objections to dealing with the institution under another brand, employees were fiercely opposed. In addition, IT operations could not be integrated sufficiently quickly to deliver the same level of service under one brand to all customers. As a result the re-branding was put on hold to be reviewed at a later stage when operations and employees were prepared for such a move. It is, therefore, advisable to identify and assess the economic value implications of the branding decision in a merger or acquisition. This does not only refer to the question which brand to use but also how this move is implemented and communicated. AXA, a global financial services group from France, acquired a range of insurance and asset management firms around the world. The re-branding was carefully assessed and executed to ensure that the brand value of the group was maximized. In markets where the acquired brands were weak, the re-branding was executed relatively quickly. In markets where the acquired brands were strong, a slow transition from endorsement by the AXA brand to a full re-brand was executed over a period of several years. In the US the operations continued to use their original brand. Another financial services example is the ING Group which re-branded all its international operation under the ING brand but in its home market in the Netherlands it kept its strong brand portfolio which included Postbank for a considerable time until it was much later re-branded ING. Vodafone is another example of a company that carefully assessed the value creation of its acquired brands. Many operations such as in Germany and Italy were co-branded with the Vodafone brand for many years before their names disappeared and were fully Vodafone branded.

The key in assessing the re-branding of a merged or acquired business is to quantify the economic impact of the different branding options – this includes the brand impact on customers, employees relative to the marketing synergies, and cost savings they can produce. The results can be quite surprising and contrary to the intuitive judgment. The Japanese electronics and IT company Fujitsu acquired ICL in the UK in 1990. Management in the UK and Japan were convinced that the ICL brand was crucial for employees and customers in particular the government which represented one of the top 10 accounts. Only after a careful economic assessment of the value creation of both brands with respect to both stakeholder groups it emerged that the Fujitsu brand provided more economic value and the ICL brand had become obsolete. As a result of this review the business was re-branded as Fujitsu Services.[6]

As brands account for a significant portion of corporate wealth and in many cases constitute the most valuable assets in the business, an assessment of their economic wealth creation is crucial to ensure optimal proceeds and outcomes from M&A transactions. The brand valuation method established in this text is well suited to deliver such an assessment. It can assess the revenue and profit generation of brands as well as their sustainability and growth potential. Such valuation process is crucial to ensure the best deal in planning and execution. Although brand valuation is a derivative method from business valuation it will deliver specific value insights that are not captured by the traditional valuations performed by investment bankers, consultants, and accountants. There are many cases where sellers have undersold their businesses due to a lack of understanding and quantification of the value of the brand assets involved. On the other side, many buyers overpay for companies as they overestimate brand and cost synergies in a transaction. Even after a transaction has been agreed there are branding issues that are best decided on the basis of a valuation of the different branding options of the combined units, most notably which brand(s) should be kept and which retired. Only a robust analysis and valuation will ensure that brand assets are optimized and brand value destruction prevented. The valuation of the brand(s) will also help in the purchase price allocation which is now required by all relevant accounting standards.

CHAPTER 11

BRAND LICENSING

Brand royalties or licenses have become an important source of brand value creation. The size of the global licensing market was estimated to amount to about US$187 billion in 2008.[1] Brand licensing is one of the fastest growing sectors in the licensing industry. Licensing is a contractual agreement in which the owner of a trademark grants permission to a third party for the economic use of the brand. In exchange for granting the rights of a brand to a licensee, the licensor obtains financial remuneration – known as the royalty. On average, royalty payments are between approximately 5 and 15 percent of the wholesale price of each sold product depending on the industry. Luxury and strong consumer brands can command a royalty fee at the higher end. Brands are licensed in categories and markets including: consumer goods; luxury goods; retailing; telecommunications; and many B2B categories.

There are three main rationales for brand licensing. The first is to earn additional returns on the use of the brand assets. The brand owner or licensor receives a return without further capital investment. In most cases the additional use does not require significant management involvement for the licensor. The second is to use licensing as a marketing tool for reaching specific audiences with little or no additional investments. If properly executed licensing can help to build and maintain the brand's core values and associations beyond the core product area.

For the licensee the brand creates a return over and above its cost, i.e., the royalty, as it provides market access and revenues that would not be possible without the brand. The use of an established brand name can help create immediate consumer awareness and reinforce brand association quickly and cost effectively, without the need for major investment required for a full-scale new brand launch. The licensee focuses his main efforts on the commercial exploitation of the revenues minus the license fee. In many cases this situation becomes more complex when the licensee is required to take on brand investments such as costs for marketing and advertising. In such a situation the licensee takes on some brand management tasks. Both parties benefit as the brand owner receives a return from markets and applications he is not willing to invest in himself and the licensee receives a revenue stream from which a return can be earned.

The third rationale for brand licensing is the exchange of intellectual property including trademarks between related parties typically headquarters and operating companies of multinational concerns. Most multinationals develop and manage their IP from their headquarters. This is particulary true for the brand which has to be managed from the centre. For the management of the brand, headquarters charge a royalty to the subsidiary companies for the use of the brand. As the royalty reduces the taxable income of the subsidiary company the local tax authority loses the tax income on the royalty. For that purpose there are rules and regulations about the transfer pricing of the use of intangible assets. As multinational companies operate in different countries with different tax rates and the amount of internal IP has increased significantly, transfer pricing and the related tax implications has become an important tool in minimizing the overall tax bill of these companies. Transfer pricing has become a complex affair and requires companies to maintain an on-going dialogue and negotiate agreements with the different local tax authorities. At the same time, tax authorities require companies to charge related parties for the use of shared assets.

The need of multinational companies to establish transfer pricing mechanisms has resulted in sophisticated tax planning and management strategies. Many globally operating businesses have organized their intellectual property into special purpose vehicles (SPVs). These SPVs have initially emerged to take advantage of different tax positions within the group. If, for example, a company has significant tax credits on a consolidated basis it needs to increase its taxable profits to utilize them. So, if headquarters starts charging its operating companies around the world a royalty for the use of the brand, taxable profits are reduced abroad and repatriated to headquarters to increase the consolidated profits which can be set off against the tax credits. Another approach is to establish the SPV in a low tax environment such as the Bahamas, Switzerland, or other tax shelters. This reduces the overall tax bill of the group as taxable profits are reduced by royalty payments for the use of the brand which are then transferred to the low tax environment where they are taxed at a lower rate. Not surprisingly, tax authorities around the world try to ensure that as much tax as possible is paid in their specific jurisdiction which has led to international rules on transfer pricing. The choice of the transfer price will affect the allocation of the total profit among the parts of the company. This is a major concern for fiscal authorities who worry that multinational entities may set transfer prices on cross-border transactions to reduce taxable profits in their jurisdiction. This has led to the rise of transfer pricing regulations and enforcement, making transfer pricing a major tax compliance issue for multinational companies.[2] As these are reasonably complex, many accounting and consulting firms have established significant practices dealing with this issue. As national tax authorities are keen to maximize their tax income companies need to be able to demonstrate a robust case that justifies charging subsidiary companies for the use of IP such as brands. This requires having clear and solid documentation on reasoning and amount for the brand royalty. One of the key issues is to prove that the royalty charge is not just a tax planning exercise but is grounded in operational necessity. For that reason many multinationals have consolidated their central marketing and brand team in an SPV and thus converted the marketing and brand function from a cost to a profit centre. The brand SPV receives the brand royalties for managing all central and strategic brand aspects such as corporate identity, brand guidelines, global brand image campaigns and PR initiatives, sponsorships, product innovation, trademark protection, issue and management of licenses, and overall brand guardianship. This structure is used for consumer brands as well as corporate brands. Companies such as Nestlé, Shell, BP, Tata, and BAT operate such functions in different versions.

SPVs are also set up to provide cheaper financing by securing the loan through the royalties income from the licensing of the brand. An example is the DB Master Finance LLC transaction, which securitized the franchise fees of the Dunkin' Donuts, Baskin Robbins and Togo's brands raising a total of US$1.7 billion in proceeds (see also Chapter 9).

ASSESSING FAIR BRAND ROYALTIES

One key issue in licensing brands is to assess an appropriate charge for the use of the brand asset that fairly reflects the inputs and benefits from licensor and licensee. There are two distinctively different brand licensing situations. The first one is the licensing transactions between independent parties. In this case, all arrangements including the royalty rate are settled by negotiation between both parties. The second one is the transaction between related parties who also legally agree the terms of the licensing arrangement including the brand royalty. However, if such arrangements have an impact on the taxable profits of one of the parties the brand royalty needs to be justified to a third party which is the tax authorities of the jurisdiction in which the tax income is reduced by the payment of the brand royalty. Although the tax assessment may have a time delay of many years companies need to agree and negotiate the royalty charged with the tax authorities. Even if the royalty has already been agreed with the tax authorities its fairness and validity will most likely be revisited after a couple of years. Equally a change in the brand royalty in the context of an existing agreement will have to be justified and agreed with the tax authorities. Although both licensing situations require a diligent preparation and documentation the internal licensing situation requires a clear explanation and justification for the royalties charged. This requires more emphasis on the economic logic of the calculation of the royalty rates. The sole focus of the royalty rate calculation for an agreement of two independent parties is to agree on a number that both parties regard as beneficial for their business. In the case of a group internal transaction the royalty rate needs to have a clear economic explanation to be accepted by the tax authorities.

In any licensing agreement the royalty rate is the most important component as it captures the monetary exchange for the use of the asset licensed. While two independent parties are free to negotiate the royalty at their will, dependent parties in transfer pricing or internal licensing need to follow agreed guidelines by national and international tax agreements. The OECD guidelines on transfer pricing prefer the profit-split (PS) method and the transactional net margin method (TNMM) although other methods that deliver a reasonable arm's length transfer price are allowed. The OECD and various tax authorities (including the IRS) acknowledge that transaction-based methods do not provide the perfect solution and that the "profit-split method" represents a suitable alternative to assessing licensing rates.[3] The profit split approach is based on the recognition that licensing intellectual property reflects a joint engagement in economic activity yielding a joint benefit. The profit split should reflect the relative contribution of the licensee and licensor and should result in a "fair return" for both parties. It is, therefore, the most comprehensive and accurate method for determining royalties for the use of brand assets.

Brand royalties are best assessed relative to the specific value creation (actual and potential) of the brand in the markets and applications in which it is licensed. The brand differs from most other intangible assets in that its value creation depends entirely on being different and unique. The economic task of the brand is to attract consumers through a differentiated and relevant offer. This economic benefit is determined through the Brand Impact analysis described in Chapter 7. The Brand Impact is the reason why a licensee is interested in paying a royalty for the use of the brand. It is therefore important that the royalty rate reflects the unique value creation of the brand.

Royalties can also be assessed by looking at royalties that have been agreed for the use of comparable brands in comparable markets. There are several databases that provide details about royalty rates and agreements. The problem with this approach lies in the need for comparability. The brand, the application, the market, and the situation of both parties need to be comparable. However, comparison of reported rates is often problematic, as many cover the use of a bundle of intangible assets that also includes the brand. This limits the use of many reported rates. Where a transaction is not directly comparable, a detailed understanding of the transaction is required so that adjustments can be made to achieve a genuine comparison. The use of the same brand in other categories and markets is not comparable just because it is the same brand being used. In order to be comparable, market and application need to be similar. Transactions relating to other applications cannot be considered "comparable" if the products rely on different functional and emotional attributes in their appeal to customers. Brand impact on customer choice differs by market and application. This influences the level of royalty that a licensee would expect to pay for the use of a brand.

In reality it is rare to find satisfactory comparable royalty rates for brands because of the unique nature of these assets. A great deal of judgment is required in deciding which rates are comparable. The range of royalties in the same category can easily differ by more than 100 percent. The value difference between the Coca-Cola and Pepsi-Cola brands is a good example for demonstrating how different the value of two brands that are similar in most aspects, except their brand values and associations, can be. Although comparable royalties is a convenient and frequently used method is should not be the primary approach for determining appropriate brand royalties. The primary approach should always be profit-split specific for the brand to be licensed.

Comparable rates albeit carefully selected can be used as cross-check for the derived royalties. RoyaltySource intellectual property database provides details on licensing transactions and royalty rates from public financial records, news releases, and other articles and references.

For assessing brand royalties the author suggests using three of the steps from the brand valuation framework described in Chapter 7. The key steps are:

1. Financial analysis: This requires identifying and quantifying the revenue and profit potential of the market and application to which the brand is licensed.
2. Brand impact: This analysis assesses the impact the brand has on generating revenues and profits in the licensed application.
3. Brand royalty calculation: Based on the brand impact analysis and the derived brand earnings, the fair royalties for the use of the brand are calculated.

Financial analysis

Before licensor and licensee can agree on a royalty they need to have an understanding about the revenue and profit potential of the brand in the licensed application and market. Both parties, therefore, need to agree on the potential of the brand to generate revenues and profits. A forecast of revenues based on historical data for the brand in its current markets and applications, the growth forecast for the category and market in which the brand license will be used, an assessment of distribution channels and customer perception and behaviors needs to be established. The revenues from the brand license are called brand license revenues (BLR). Although the projection should fit the period of the royalty agreement there needs to be sufficient maneuvering space to adjust the forecasts to the actual revenue development. From the revenues all operating costs and a charge for the capital employed are subtracted to determine the likely economic profit called intangible earnings (IE) from the licensed operations. In situations in which historical or forecast financial information is not obtainable the royalty will be based on the brand impact analysis and then adjusted according to actual financials. The main purpose of the financial analysis is to establish the economic value potential of the brand as a basis for splitting the returns between licensor and licensee.

101

Brand impact (BI)

The brand impact (BI) analysis determines which portion of the intangible earnings is attributable to the brand. In some strongly brand-driven businesses such as perfumes the brand impact is very high as the brand is the predominant driver and asset of the business. In more technically complex businesses, the ability to earn in excess of a base return on tangible assets is only partly a function of the brand in addition to other intangible assets such as personal contacts, technologies, management expertise, sales forces, databases, distribution agreements, etc. The brand impact analysis (see Chapter 7) determines the degree to which the brand is a driver of the customer demand and purchase decisions. The purpose of the brand impact analysis is to identify the specific contribution the brand makes in influencing customer choice and thus intangible earnings. By applying the brand impact percentage to the intangible earnings, the brand earnings (BE), as basis for the royalty calculation, are derived. The BE represent the total return attributable to the brand asset. In cases where the licensee does not build the brand beyond the standard operational activities such as marketing the given brand content and distribution that was valued and considered in the financial royalties assessment the brand earnings represent the economic benefit due to the provider of the brand, i.e., the licensor. This is the appropriate approach in licensing situations where the licensor provides all the brand content and its strategic execution and the licensee uses the brand to derive earnings from operational activities such as manufacturing, distribution, and management. This is the case in most brand licensing situations such as those of luxury and consumer brands.

Brand contribution (BC)

In some complex licensing situations where the brand building depends on the implementation in the licensed market it may be necessary to split the brand earnings between licensor and licensee according to their direct contribution in building the brand. This is typically the case in some B2B or corporate brand licensing situations where the licensee manages the implementation of the brand in its market. This is often the case in the internal licensing of corporate brands within multinational companies where the head office provides brand guidelines and strategic support but a significant quantity of brand management has to be executed locally at the operating company level. In such transfer pricing situations many tax authorities require a clear economic rationale for the amount of the brand royalty and the recognition of the local operating company in the building of the brand. Brand contribution analysis is a structured process for splitting the brand earnings in a way that provides the licensee with an incentive to manage the brand in a responsible manner, while providing the licensor with a fair return on the brand. The brand earnings are split between licensor and licensee according to the contribution each party makes to the overall brand impact on customers' purchase drivers. This analysis is performed for each purchase driver by splitting the brand impact between licensor and licensees. In some cases one party only contributes, in some cases both parties contribute. This assessment is based on a combination of market research and management interviews. The brand contribution approach has helped many leading companies around the world to negotiate and implement royalty agreements with third parties and tax authorities. The brand contribution of the licensee (BC_L) is then the basis for the fair brand royalty.

Brand royalty calculation

Brand royalties are calculated by multiplying the brand earnings with the brand impact and the licensee's brand contribution percentage following the formula:

Brand license revenues (BLR) = Revenues generated under the brand license

Intangible earnings (IE) = BLR − (Operating costs + charge for capital employed)

Brand earnings (BE) = IE × BI

Brand royalty (BR) = BE/BLR

In the case where the brand earnings need to be split between licensor and licensee according the brand contribution analysis the brand royalties are calculated using the following formula:

Brand royalty (BR) = (BE × BC_L))/BLR

The brand royalties calculation is based on revenues – this is the most common way of charging royalties as it is the easiest financial number for the licensor to audit and the least difficult for the licensee to manipulate. A profit related figure would be conceptionally more appropriate but is more complex to administer and more volatile than a revenue-based royalty as more inputs can affect the payment. It also makes it easier for the licensee to book the royalty as pre-tax expense. However, the analysis can also be used as a base for setting royalties as absolute numbers or as a percentage of sales volume or different profit figures before the deduction of tax at the local level. In some cases the licensor negotiates an upfront fee in addition an annual royalty payment. The royalty payment can also be adjusted to the commercial circumstances of the venture. For example, the licensor can grant delayed payments during the start-up phase or for periods in which the licensee does not generate a profit. Ultimately, the royalty rate is subject to the negotiations of two agreeing parties.

MANAGING BRAND LICENSING

Brand licensing is an attractive income for brand owners in a market which they do not intend to enter or lack the capital to enter. From a marketing perspective it can also build the brand with audiences it otherwise does not reach. Licensing the brand in other geographic markets can build awareness and brand equity for a potential later entry. However, the licensing of the brand needs to be assessed in the context of the core value drivers of the brand. Uncontrolled licensing can dilute and substantially damage the value of brands. There are many cases in which licensing has nearly destroyed the value of brands. The most prominent example is the Gucci brand in the 1980s. In seeking short-term cash flows Gucci's management issued hundreds of licenses around the world. The majority of these licenses went to the Far East – the Gucci logo started to appear on a wide range of low price items such as cheap key rings and other accessories. These low-price products did not match Gucci's luxury heritage and brand values. The prolific appearance of the Gucci logo on a cheap and low-quality product line-up had a negative effect on the brand's core luxury business. As the luxury and quality perception of Gucci declined, increasingly fewer customers bought their core products. As a result the company came to the brink of bankruptcy. One of the key elements of Del Sole and Tom Ford's legendary turnaround of the Gucci brand and its business was the repurchase and strict management control of all licenses and focus on a product line-up that represented the core values of the Gucci brand such as style, heritage, elegance, decadence, and luxury. Licensing income is still an important earning stream for Gucci but it is closely controlled by management and follows clear guidelines to ensure that it builds rather than dilutes the brand. The main product areas in which luxury brands are licensed are perfumes, sunglasses, and watches. This has extended into mobile phones, hotels, and cars. LG sells a Prada branded mobile phone and Samsung one carrying the Giorgio Armani brand. Although the base phone is identical to other products the design and software are aligned to the brands. There are also promotional licensing arrangements such as the Hermès and Smart cooperation. The tenth anniversary special edition Hermès designed and branded Smart car costs more than three times that of the base model and distribution is restricted to selected dealerships. A long-running and very successful licensing program has been Caterpillar's licensing of its brand in the apparel sector. The product range includes the famous CAT boots and matches the ruggedness of the Caterpillar brand which has earth-moving equipment as its core business. Sales of Caterpillar-licensed merchandise, including footwear, apparel, watches and scale models, amount to about US$1 billion per year.[4]

Although brand licensing is for most companies a lucrative side business there are companies focusing solely on this activity. One of the best known example is Pierre Cardin a famous designer and fashion label in the 1960s that diluted its brand equity through prolific licensing into all markets and applications. Today the brand has more than 900 licenses across 94 countries, generating an annual turnover of about US$1 billion.[5] In the US companies such as Cherokee Inc. and the Iconix brand group focus solely on the licensing of brand names and trademarks for apparel, footwear, and accessories. Although these operations are relatively small with Iconix' annual turnover at US$217 million (financial year 2008) and Cherokee's at US$ 36 million (financial year 2009) these businesses generate EBIT margins in the high 60s with staff of 82 and 20 respectively.[6] These examples provide some insight into just how profitable brand licensing can be.

Brand licensing has become a significant industry, when properly executed it can provide significant returns for licensor and licensee. While the financial return is the predominant reason for entering into licensing agreements there are also strategic management issues to be considered. This is true for licensing between two independent parties as well as dependent parties in a transfer pricing situation. In both cases it is important that the licensing activity does not devalue the core brand but helps to support and build it. The example of Gucci shows how an executed licensing without a clear strategic framework impairs the value of a prominent brand. The internal licensing of brands within multinational companies does not only provide potential tax benefits but can, if properly structured, create a stronger corporate brand and marketing function. A centralized focus on brand management raises the importance of the brand with senior management and operating companies. The centralized brand functions can be more efficient in managing global brand communications such as corporate identity, global image campaigns, and sponsorships as well as trademark protection and licensing. By making the brand function a profit centre through receiving brand royalties, marketing and branding becomes more clearly accountable. The operating companies will also manage an asset differently if they have to pay for the use of the asset instead of getting it for free and thus taking it for granted. Shell's establishment of Shell Brands International is a well-executed example of such a structure.

The assessment of the appropriate royalty rates for brand licensing requires careful analysis and reasoning in order to ensure that the brand royalties are fair and benefit both parties. For that reason the royalty rates should be calculated on the profit-split basis described above where a clear understanding and assessment of the contribution each party makes and the economic benefit it receives in return is established. The analysis and reasoning of this approach are equally beneficial for negotiating royalties between independent and dependent parties. In the case of internal brand licensing this approach is also beneficial in the negotiations with and documentation for tax authorities around the world as they often require an economic logic for setting these royalties. The comparable royalties approach is useful for cross-checking the derived results but less useful as primary approach due to the difficulty of finding reasonably comparable situations. As the value creation of brands rests in their difference to other brands comparability is principally difficult as comparability would reduce the value creation of a brand. Brand licensing is another example of the economic value creation of brands.

CHAPTER 12

THE BRAND VALUE CHAIN

The value creation of brands lies in their impact on customer purchase decisions. The manifestation of brand value is the economic value that can be derived from current and future purchases of the brand's products and services. In order to maximize the value generation of a brand it is important to understand the flow from the brand to its impact on customers' purchase decisions. This flow can be described in a brand value chain. There have been several concepts that have tried to describe and explain the relationship between brand, marketing actions, and financial outcomes. One of the most well-known academic approaches comes from Kevin L. Keller, a professor at Tuck Business School who identified a value chain consisting of four elements: marketing program investments; customer mindset; brand performance; and shareholder value.[1] While Keller's four building blocks describe the main marketing investments and metrics their interplay remains at a very top-level view. Another value chain concept is the "purchase funnel" and its derivatives which has been made famous by McKinsey but is also used by other consultancies in different variations.[2] Based on market research studies it starts with the total possible market for the brand and then analyses how many potential customers are lost at each stage of the funnel until the actual customers that buy the brand remain. Over the last couple of years the purchase funnel has been criticized for its strict linear nature. Nevertheless, it is still a widely used tool.

The brand value chain described here is based on the brand value concept and is the result of first-hand experience. The rationale for breaking up the value creation of the brand in distinctive stages is not to claim or prove straight line relationships between all stages but to provide a useful logic to identify, understand, quantify, and manage the economic value generation of a brand. This brand value chain, shown in Figure 12.1, consists of the five distinct elements: brand content;

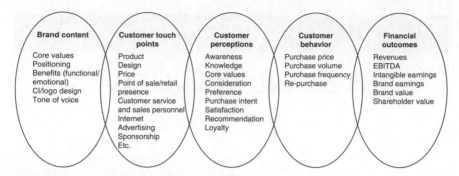

FIGURE 12.1 **The brand value chain**

customer touch points; customer perception; customer behavior; and financial outcome.

A brand consists of a set of values and associations by which it can be identified, codified, and managed. The content of the brand comprises all key elements that create perceptions about the brand in the consumers' mind including the brand name and its visual and experiential representations (logo, packaging, specific product and design features, customer service). These will immediately evoke a set of associations. For existing brands these associations are the result of a company's marketing activities and customers' experience with the brand as well as with the product(s) or service(s) it sells. Some brand associations can be very distinctive others will be similar to competitors. For example, the distinctive associations of BMW are performance, quality engineering, and style. These are not only communicated through the tag line "The Ultimate Driving Machine" but also through the overall purchase and product experience. On the perception of these attributes the brand excels relative to other car manufacturers. These associations are not just the result of the company's communication and marketing activities but of all operations that impact the customer experience including design, engineering, driving experience, and dealerships. The interaction of all business activities creates the brand perception. The brand is therefore the result of the promise and delivery of an experience. It is thus an important component and expression of business strategy.

BRAND CONTENT

The first element in the value chain is the definition of the brand content which is achieved in a positioning statement. At the core of the brand is the brand's DNA or platform which comprises the core values of the brand from which the brand's positioning core attributes and perceptions are derived. The core values are the result of the company's history, its view about the future for its markets and customers, and its capabilities to provide a differentiated and relevant offer to its customers. The core values and the resultant positioning of the brand can be altered by systematic management action. However, in order to remain credible with consumers and to be able to deliver the brand successfully the core values of a brand in most cases can only be altered gradually in order to avoid impairing the value creation of the brand. Brands, such as Coca-Cola, IBM, and Mercedes Benz are successful examples of continuity and consistency in their brand values. Some brand perceptions are the result of company operations and culture that may not have been codified or formalized at the beginning of the business but have become a *modus operandi* of the business. Microsoft, and Google are examples of brands that have emerged in this way. On the other hand, brands can also be created from scratch in particular when the image of the brand is all the customer is buying. Good examples of manufactured brands are Absolut, O_2, and Grey Goose Vodka. The brand content needs to be codified in a way that it can be communicated and applied internally as well as externally. Common pitfalls are either overly simplistic reductions of the brand essence to a tag line for the advertising campaign or overly elaborate write-ups that lack clear definition. Although refreshment is a core theme of the Coca-Cola brand, there are several more elements that define the core of the brand. The prolific use of brand consultants has resulted in many bland and exchangeable brand essence or platform statements. A useful brand essence combines the distinctive associations with the brand with the company's ability to deliver these throughout the customer experience.

The purpose of brand management is to optimize the use of the brand's core values to produce maximum financial results. The core values of a brand do not change easily as they have been the result of, and the reason for, the commercial success of the brand. Only if these values cease to represent the DNA do they need to be changed in order to reflect the new commercial reality. The brand DNA is part of a company's business strategy. In the context of business strategy, management can set these core values and the overall positioning of the brand. However, if these are not reflected in the activity and behaviors of the brand then the economic value of the brand is easily affected.

It is, after all, the brand perception of the buyers of the company's products and services that determine its commercial success. Management ambitions or mere window dressing through changes in corporate design or advertising communications are not sufficient to create sustainable brand value. A prominent example was BP's re-branding under the motto "beyond petroleum" in 2001 which was supposed to reposition the oil company as a future oriented investor in renewable energies represented by a sun like symbol as a new logo. As part of the re-brand the Amoco brand in the US was re-branded and the identity globally aligned. The investment in the communication campaign was significant. The company spent more then US$250 million just on the advertising plus the global redesign of all its petrol forecourts. The process was very well executed and resulted in significant improvements of the BP brand in consumers' perception. A consumer survey found that 21 percent of them thought BP was the "greenest" of oil companies, followed by Shell at 15 percent and Chevron at 13 percent. The campaign also won a 2007 gold Effie from the American Marketing Association. BP said that between 2000 and 2007, its brand awareness went from 4 percent to 67 percent.[3] From a pure communication perspective the "beyond petroleum" campaign was well designed and executed. However, commercial reality and the company's behavior did not match the brand's promise. Investments in renewable energies hovered at about 1 percent of the group's capital expenditure nearly as much as the spend on the advertising campaign. While many new companies were developing renewable energy solutions BP's efforts remained peripheral at best. In addition, the company's reputation was severely harmed by its handling of the explosion at one of its Texan oil refineries that killed several employees. After 8 years of "beyond petroleum" the new CEO Tony Hayward re-focused the company back on petroleum. The head of the renewable energy business resigned and the business is up for disposal through either initial public offering (IPO) or sale.[4] BP is an example where management ambition and communication strategy did not follow the business behavior and strategy. The result was a significant waste of resources and destruction of shareholder value.

A similar fate encountered British Airways as it dropped its "Britishness" to become BA and "the world's favourite airline." The re-branding was bold and expressed the airline's international ambition to be a "world citizen." However, in its home market the core of BA's customer base was less cosmopolitan, prompting the airline to bring back the

Union Jack symbol and re-focus the brand on its British heritage. Again, shareholders did not benefit from this venture.

Coca-Cola's experiment with New Coke is another example where management strategy tried to stray from the brand's core by introducing a new and improved formula. While blind tasting and market research may have suggested that consumers preferred the newly engineered taste, the effect on the brand was devastating. The company had fiddled with the original and secret formula which formed part of the myth of being the original cola drink. Luckily, the brand was strong enough to survive and today New Coke is a distant memory and a case study on how not to re-position a brand. How strong and powerful the core values of brands can be, if properly managed and communicated is demonstrated by brands such as Coca-Cola, Nike, Apple, Kellogg, Gillette, IBM, Nivea, and BMW that have developed iconic brand status through sticking to their core values. These brands have not changed the core values of their brands for many decades. Even the re-launch of the Mini by the BMW group focused on the core value of the Mini brand first communicated in the 1960s.

The values and their communication need to be adapted to market conditions and sentiment. The Marlboro cigarette brand was initially marketed to female consumers. Its breakthrough success however came with the repositioning as a macho cigarette with cowboy imagery. The Marlboro man became one of the leading brand icons in marketing history. The DNA of consumer brands which are mainly driven by communications can be more easily changed than the DNA of a corporate brand where the whole organization needs to follow by aligning communications and behaviors. That can mean changing the emphasis of the values or the way they are expressed in communications and through company behavior. For example, the financial crisis of 2008/9 has made stability and trust an important value for many financial services brands. Although most brands had this in their DNA it had been de-emphasized as customers perceived all banks to be safe. The crisis changed this and re-focused banks' attention to communicate trust as a core value.

Communication and emphasis of the core values may change to adapt to changing market conditions and Zeitgeist. A successful brand meets a customer need in a relevant and clearly differentiated manner from its competitors. Relevant means that it is obtainable for the target audience. Customers may not be aware of the need but realize it when confronted with the offer. Sony's Walkman and Apple's i-pod are good examples of such solution-driven needs.

Brands can also be created from scratch in particular if the actual product is indistinguishable from many others as is often the case with vodka. Brands such as Absolut and Grey Goose were newly created brands without heritage or history. Selling vodka from Sweden or France was not an obvious concept as both markets lacked global recognition for vodka heritage. Absolut was the first brand that addressed the premium segment of the global vodka market. The concept of purity and premium was nicely packaged in an advertising campaign and a distinctive bottle. It hit strong consumer demand and has become one of the most valuable spirits brands. As the premium vodka category matured the super premium segment emerged. The Grey Goose brand was created in 2000 and its super premium position was carried by the fact that it originated from France, which for the American consumers was a clear sign of premium. In the telecommunication market, the Orange and O_2 brands are good examples for engineered brands that have become very successful. In 2007, Orange became the operating brand for all of France Telecom's activities. These examples illustrate that successful brands can be created from scratch. However, among the leading 100 global brands about 70 percent have been in use for more than 50 years with the younger brands having developed mostly in new categories such as IT and the Internet. The majority of these brands have emerged from a combination of communications and behaviors.

CUSTOMER TOUCH POINTS

Customer touch points represent all key contact points between the company and the market. Once the brand positioning is defined it needs to be communicated and delivered through all customer relevant touch points which are the second link in the brand value chain. Management actions need to focus initiatives and investments on the customer touch point delivery of the brand. All relevant business functions that have a direct and visible effect on the customer experience need to be aligned to the brand positioning. The brand positioning needs to be used as a framework for their specific activities. Marketing and sales need to ensure that all communications follow the strategic brand positioning in look, feel, and content. This includes pricing strategies, advertising, Internet presence, sponsorships, sales and product brochures, packaging, channel and point of sale presence, corporate identity, tone of voice, brand architecture or managing the relationship of different brands as well as any other communication materials such as employee and investor relations materials. In the case of a multinational company this requires coordination and supervision of the operations in each country. While headquarters provides strategic direction, guidelines, and have ultimate responsibility for managing the brand, local marketing functions need to have sufficient flexibility to adjust to their specific market conditions. An advertising campaign for a shampoo that shows a lady washing her hair in a small lake under a waterfall in an exotic location may communicate natural beauty and ingredients as well as freedom in the western world, however: in the developing world such a scene will be interpreted as poor, unsophisticated, old-fashioned, and unclean. That means the same brand values can require different communications to address the interpretations of different market conditions and sentiments. These cultural differences are, in particular, important for brands that want to be seen as part of the local fabric. In many markets consumers have little awareness that Colgate or Mars are large global brands. Overall, most leading global brands are successful due to their consistency across all communications and touch points. Apple, BMW, and Gillette are examples of brands that have very successfully established a consistent global brand appearance at all levels. The brand positioning also needs to guide and direct product design and development as well as R&D to ensure that products and services reinforce the core brand values. This does not mean that the creativity of researchers and engineers is constrained but it indicates that efforts must focus on the largest value enhancing opportunities. VW's Phaeton is an example for a product that does not fit with the values of the VW brand such as simplicity and affordability. Not surprisingly it has been one of the biggest flops in recent car history. Samsung provides its R&D team with strategic brand guidance to ensure that efforts are focused on brand-aligned products and services.[5] On the other hand R&D can be the source of products and services that create leading global brands such as HP, Intel, Microsoft, Apple, and Google.

Brands that do not have direct access to the end-user/buyer need to focus on product, communications, and the service they offer because these are the touch points that a company can manage and influence. There are also several co-marketing efforts such as in-store promotions, point-of-sale, and shelf management where the brand owner can assert influence albeit at a lower level of control. While marketing communications and product development, which are to large extent closely related, are important many companies have embraced a more holistic view of branding beyond the traditional marketing functions. This is, in particular, the case for service companies or companies that have direct control over a significant part of their distribution though retail outlets, direct sales forces, the Internet, and telephone sales. For example, Hermès and Tiffany sell solely through controlled retail outlets such as their own shops, company-controlled and branded concession stores, and the Internet. Apple generates about 15 percent of its sales through its own branded stores. Oracle, IBM, GE, and Accenture generate all of their sales through a direct sales force. Amazon, eBay, lastminute.com, and expedia.com sell only via the Internet. In these cases the additional customer touch points need to be integrated into the brand experience. The retail environment of an Apple or Hermès shop is a key purchase enhancing factor. This has implication for shop design, materials use, shop lay-out, and store location. In addition, the look and behavior of the shop assistant is another important brand touch point. A shop assistant in an Apple store will look and behave differently to a shop assistant in a Hermès shop. The retail brand Abercrombie & Fitch have clear requirements for their customer-facing personnel to consolidate the "healthy" appearance of their advertising models.

To optimize these customer touch points, human resource (HR) departments need brand guidelines for selecting, training, and managing sales personnel and managers in a way that will enhance the perception of the brand and support the sale of branded goods and services. Even if the customer interaction is confined to the telephone the tone of voice, waiting time, and handling of complaints or orders are important elements of the customer experience particularly if there is no other human interaction. For example, Virgin mobile has developed, in the UK, a particular and distinctive tone of voice that fits with its core brand value of being young, unconventional, and the customer's champion.

For most B2B and service brands their employees are the most important customer touch point. The appearance and behavior of a relationship manager or consultant from companies such as IBM, GE, or Accenture has a significant impact on the client perception of the brand. Many companies have recognized that their brand values need to be an integrated part of the personnel recruitment, development, and management process. To successfully engage employees requires a close alignment of the brand communication process with the other corporate processes such as recruitment, people development, and organization. An isolated communications campaign lecturing employees about brand values that is not organizationally relevant has little impact and can render such an exercise trivial. On the other hand if the employees have been made strong advocates then this can substantially enhance sale and delivery of the company's products and services. Employee alignment enhances product development, R&D, sales, and customer service management.[6] In order to foster this process the brand can be integrated into the remuneration process of employees. At many companies, such as Samsung Electronics, senior executives are partly remunerated according to brand value creation. The chairman sets brand value targets the achievement of which became part of the promotion and bonus process. The integration of brand value into the remuneration process directly rewards brand building and alignment of employees.

Although this ultimately involves all parts of the business, the customer-facing operations are relatively more important in delivering the brand. In service organizations a relatively larger part of the organization is involved in the brand as more employees have direct interaction with the customer. A consumer brand such as Coca-Cola or Nivea is not delivered by the employees as these products are sold through intermediaries and the company's employees rarely interact with the consumers of the product.

In service or retail delivered brands a dedicated part of the employees interact directly with the consumer or customer although the Internet has become an increasingly important brand delivery point. A financial service brand is delivered through branches and telephone centers and a retail brand through the sales personnel. Brand promise and delivery are not limited to communications such as design, advertising, and messaging but involve other operations such as R&D, customer service, and sales. Some are better at communication and delivering their brand through operational and product excellence than through traditional marketing communications like advertising. For example, Samsung Electronics has made a deliberate effort to put their brand positioning at the core of their product design and development as well as their channel marketing efforts. Once the brand positioning is agreed it needs to become an essential part of the whole operation in particular of all customer focusing functions such as product development, distribution, customer service, sales, and communications to ensure a consistent brand delivery through all customer touch points. In order to build its premium image in the US Samsung pulled distribution of its mobile phones from Wal-Mart and focused only on specialized stores. The Apple brand is consistently implemented throughout the organization. Products, pricing, communications, investor presentations, trade shows, the Apple stores, and resellers form a consistent experience of the Apple brand. The more consistently the brand communications and experience are executed through all touch points the stronger the impact on existing and potential consumers of the brand. The main customer touch points are communications, product, design, customer service, point of sale, retail environment, and price. Consistency ensures that each piece of communication and experience reinforces the same brand message thus increasing its impact.

The alignment and optimization of all brand touch points delivers a strong and consistent brand message to existing and potential customers. These brand communications and experiences create and impact demand from consumers. If they are properly orchestrated and delivered effectively, the brand's values will be understood by consumers and impact their purchase decisions. In a media and message cluttered world a company's brand communications needs to be as focused and as consistent as possible to be able to affect customers' purchases. Apple and BMW are good examples of such an integrated approach. Product design, function delivery, experience, advertising, point of sale, packaging, and after-sales service operate as a seamless process that elevates the companies products beyond their functional benefits to a unique offer that can charge customers prices that go far beyond the delivery of the tangible product features.

CUSTOMER PERCEPTIONS

The next link in the brand value chain reflects the impact of management actions and touch point execution on the perception of actual and potential consumers. The combined brand touch points can create a virtuous cycle of brand awareness, deeper knowledge, integration into the consideration set, purchase, repurchase, and recommendation to others. These activities are not linear, they occur simultaneously which makes their coordination and consistency even more important. The perceptions and associations consumers have about the brand are the result. The key metrics for assessing customer perceptions are the quality of awareness (prompted, un-prompted, top of mind), knowledge (details about the brand's offer), differentiation (to competing offers), relevance (price point, offer), performance on core values and delivery (consumers view on how the brand performs against its claims), consideration, preference, purchase intent, satisfaction, recommendation, and re-purchase intent. These so-called brand equity metrics measure and assess a brand consumers' perceptions of the brand and their intended purchase behavior. They also assess how close or far potential customers are from purchasing the brand.

CUSTOMER BEHAVIORS

While brand perceptions are important they need to convert to purchases to be commercially relevant and effective. This leads to the next link in the brand value chain – consumer behavior. The brand communication and experience impacts customers' perceptions about the brand and what it offers. These perceptions drive consumer behavior. The higher the relevance and the differentiation of the brand the stronger its impact on consumers' purchase decisions that then result in price, volume, and frequency of purchase. The purpose of brand management is to increase the number of customers buying more of the company's products and services more frequently at the highest price possible. Customer behavior materializes at the point of purchase (direct or intermediary) through purchase price, volume and frequency, as well as re-purchase.

FINANCIAL OUTCOMES

Consumers' purchase behavior produces the revenues of the business from which its extracts profits and ultimate value for its shareholders or owners. The brand impact is a continuous process which produces an on-going stream of cash flows. Brand communications and experience ensure that customers purchase the brand again and again thereby creating a loyal customer base. At their best, brand perceptions create a mental monopoly with a large customer base that no longer considers other brands. This then produces a sustainable earnings stream. The historic and future expected cash flows derived from the brand build the basis for analysts' and investors' assessment of the company's share price. This is where the brand fulfils its ultimate role in creating sustainable shareholder value.

If the brand communication and delivery provide a relevant and differentiated offer the right audience will buy the brand and, depending on the emotional connection with the brand, create a deep and sustained bond between the brand, its offer, and the consumer. Apple, BMW, Harley-Davidson, Coca-Cola, Porsche, Louis Vuitton, Chanel, and Gillette are just a few examples of brands that have, through consistent and focused brand touch point management, created such a strong bond with their consumers that many would not seriously consider another brand. These brands have created a "mental monopoly" within consumers' mind that ensures a loyal customer base. This psychological impact triggers behaviors that produce a financial result for the company. The psychologically triggered purchase of the brand's offer results in consumers' behavior towards the brand. The brand's offer is considered and the consumer purchases what they believe is the right mix of functional and emotional benefits. From the revenues created through consumer purchases the business extracts profits and value for shareholders. The level and predictability of demand for the brand's goods and services result in relatively higher returns (for example, EBITDA, operating cashflow) at relatively lower risk (for example, beta) which translate into superior shareholder value generation.

BRAND MANAGEMENT IMPACT

The brand value chain is not only a useful tool in identifying and understanding the value creation of brands from conception to value creation. It is also a way of managing the value creation of a brand. Each element of the chain has a distinctive function: Definition of the brand DNA; communication and delivery of the brand through all defined touch points; brand reception by consumers according to perception of functional and emotional benefits; and behavior through purchase price and volume, financial impact through revenues, cashflow, and sustainable shareholder value. The functions can be managed and optimized according to their impact on value creation. Through cause-and-effect modeling, the relationships between the different elements and impact on value creation of each element can be identified, assessed, and measured. This provides clear management guidance on which brand element creates most value, touch point hierarchy according to value creation, and the economic outcome of consumers brand perceptions. The model can also be used to hypothesize the effect of different brand strategies such as which touch point or brand message should be emphasized to optimize brand value. This has a direct implication on brand investments. The framework can assess the return on investment of the different brand elements. The budget allocation process becomes better grounded in value creation and direct economic impact.

The brand value chain describes the economic impact of the brand on the company's value creation. It identifies each key element, its function, and impact within the value chain. It therefore provides a formidable management tool and framework for quantifying the return on brand investments. The brand value chain embeds the brand within the company's operations.

THE EMPLOYEE BRAND VALUE CHAIN

While the main value creation of the brand is based on revenue generation from customers it can also impact other stakeholders of the business such as employees, the general public, investors, and regulatory institutions albeit to very different degrees. To these stakeholders the brand communicates and delivers a different offer than to customers. Some companies have created employer brands that attract the best available talent. Throughout all employment levels a corporate brand can be an important factor to obtain the best available workforce. While this is important for all businesses it is vital for a service business where the main brand delivery is through its employees. This is the case for companies such as IBM, Accenture, GE, Goldman Sachs, Microsoft, and SAP. These companies are therefore keen to attract the best available talent to their businesses. A key consideration for many employees, in particular so called knowledge workers, next to remuneration is development and training as well as the status of the employer's brand. The attraction of the employer brand is derived from its perception of its success in its chosen markets.

In addition and often related the company's market reputation employee specific factors such as compensation, development potential and career opportunities, training, work environment, and the CV appeal of the brand are driving employee choice. It obviously depends on the economic environment and the attractiveness of the skill-set

119

of the specific employees. In recessionary times job safety and salary dominate choice. However, with people-driven businesses dominating the economies in the developed world the "war on talent" is an on-going theme within most companies. The brand is therefore an important aspect for people desiring to work for a specific company. Employee specific elements can emerge from a business's operations. Having learned at or worked for a blue chip company adds value to nearly all CVs. In addition some companies are better known for their training, people development, earnings potential, and corporate culture. For many years Google has been one of the preferred choices of graduates. Companies such as GE, Goldman Sachs, Microsoft, BMW, McKinsey, BCG, PwC, Toyota, and Tata, to name a few, attract the best graduates because of the benefits they offer employees. In the US the top employment choices for graduates are leading brands such as Google, BCG, and Goldman Sachs. However, the brand impact on employees is different to consumers as they are experiencing the brand on a daily basis for 8 hours or more. This means that discrepancies between promise and delivery are easily detected. In addition, functional and material benefits are key drivers for employees. Even blue chip brands such as Goldman Sachs, BCG, and McKinsey not only offer great training and development opportunities but also above peer group financial compensation. Despite the attraction of blue chip brands the actual brand experience at the workplace can change perceptions and favor lesser known brands and companies. The 2008 result for Fortune's best places to work includes in the top 25 only nine well-known brands. It indicates that a strong brand attracts top talent but that overall employee's appreciation is driven by the actual experience which may differ from the overall market reputation. Nevertheless, work culture and employee endorsement can be significant brand and business value drivers. Some of the fastest growing global brands have been built on their work culture without the use of any paid advertising. Google and Starbucks are the result of their superior employee attraction and perception. Google attracts the most creative talent that expands the depth of application and thus the brand. Starbucks lives off the experience delivered by its baristas and other staff. Both organizations have built the value of their brands through a strong focus on employee engagement and work culture. At Starbucks the employees are at the core of the brand delivery. They way they treat customers and make the coffee is key to the experience in-store. Starbucks ran into operational problems when the company accelerated store openings but did not maintain high-quality staff selection and training. This resulted in poor customer experiences in many of the newly-opened stores. As a result the company's CEO Howard Schultz implemented store closures and slowed down the pace of expansion to ensure that all Starbucks stores can deliver the brand experience and live up to the brand's reputation. McDonald's have made significant efforts in building their brand with employees. They have established internal training and career development programs to shake off the "McJobs" image and in the UK have even been awarded their own qualifications equal to GCSEs, A levels, and degrees, in subjects such as fast-food restaurant management.[7] That means McDonald's employees can, if they so wish, receive a degree from the company. The other positive effect is that employees feel cared for and start developing pride in working at McDonald's. That is quite a shift in perception. Employee engagement and branding cannot only benefit a company internally but also externally. The link between employee engagement and business outcomes is well established. Employee engagement results in lower turnover rates, higher advocacy of the company and its products, and extra efforts to please customers. In many companies employees are also the window to customers.[8]

The success metrics for the brand impact on employees is the level of qualifications of employees, turnover rates, productivity, revenues and EBITDA per employee. In order to align employees with the brand, companies must design corporate brand values which need to be communicated and implemented throughout the organization including recruitment and management. The brand values need to be part of the performance review and affect promotions as well as compensation. However, the brand values need to be relevant and not just paid lip service. Credibility is fundamental in making brand engagement with employees work. They experience the brand every day and can immediately detect whether it is just communication or reality.

THE INVESTOR BRAND VALUE CHAIN

Another group that is affected by the corporate or organizational brand are investors. However, their reliance on brand operates very differently from other stakeholders. Investors recognize that strong brands attract consumers and customers that generate revenues from which shareholder value is extracted. This is, in particular, true for consumer-facing businesses and traditional consumer brand conglomerates such as The Coca-Cola Company, P&G, Nestlé, Unilever, Baierdorf, and PepsiCo. In these businesses brands are the key drivers of their financial success. However, for assessing value creation and investment decisions they rely on the analysis of financial data such as revenue growth, EBITDA margin, free cash flow, ROE, price to book values, and P/E ratios. These are historically available for all publicly-traded companies and are analyzed with complex statistical models to identify trends. However, the golden rule is that past performance is insufficient to predict future performance. The investment decision to buy a stock of a company is based on the expectation of future value creation which consists of appreciation of the share price and dividend payments. That means that investors rely on a future promise of cash flows when making investment decisions. The assessment of this promise is based in most cases on sophisticated quantitative analyses of past performance, economic and industry data as well company specific information. Equity analysts produce detailed reports and make recommendations regarding share prices. However, the years 2008 and 2009 demonstrated that despite all the analytical sophistication, analysts and fund managers failed to anticipate and adjust to one of the worst stock market crashes in economic history. With very few exceptions fund managers lost a fortune throughout 2008 and at the beginning of 2009. Before the crisis unfolded some very prominent economists and analysts predicted that the S&P 500 index would rise again in 2008 just before it nosedived. This clearly shows that despite the detailed analyses and sophisticated statistics the vast majority of analysts, economists, and investors were completely taken by surprise by the crisis. Forecasts and historic analysis are very valuable tools but ultimately they cannot predict the future. Future cash flows are what investors are buying when they buy shares in quoted companies. Here strong brands provide comfort as they enhance the likelihood of future cash flows. Although analysts and institutional investors base their investment decision on detailed financial assessments strong brands provide a certain level of backup and guarantee because in the end it is hard to predict future cash flow. The main effect of brands on investors is the financial results they produce. There is also the security they provide based on the proven effect they have demonstrated. It is therefore little surprise that shares of companies with strong brands outperform their peers. They do so because they provide better and more predictable financial results. Investors trust the brand but only with proof of their financial success.

So in order to impress investors with brands companies need to demonstrate what cash flows they can produce. There can be situations when brand value can help in investor communications. Orange, in the first year after their flotation on the London stock exchange, then only operating in the UK, used the value of their brand to demonstrate to investors that despite negative cash flows they were investing in and building a strong brand that in the near future would produce positive cash flows. This helped to convince investors and stabilized the share price at a crucial moment for the company. Orange became a leading brand in the UK mobile network market and delivered not only strong cash flows but a very high share price when sold to France Telecom. The brand was so strong and attractive that many years later France Telecom decided to re-brand all its major operations in all its markets to Orange. There are several companies that have used the financial value of this brand to demonstrate to investors that they are buying the shares of a company with a strong brand. Samsung, Intel, Philips, and The Coca-Cola Co. have stated or referred in their communications, including annual reports, to the value of their brand as a sign of the strength of their operations and the sustainability of their cash flows. Investors are happy to see a strong brand but they need the proof that this brand can deliver the expected future cash flows. As such investors will always rely on financial analyses for making investment decisions. Their view on the future performance of the business is positively supported by a strong brand. Companies can use the value of their brand(s) to reassure investors about the future performance of the business but they will need to deliver in the long run and in most cases they have. The brand value chain for investors works through the financial results generated by the branded business. A strong brand lends credibility to the outlook of the business, expansion of the company into new products and markets as well as some guarantee for future cash flows. Apple is a good example where investor's belief next to technology and management in the brand supports their valuation of future cash flows. However, if revenues, EBITDA, and cash flows do not match investors' expectations the share price will be immediately affected.

Ultimately, the brand value communication with investors is only effective through the delivery of key financial data. That is the reason why investor relations focus on the communication of these items. Nevertheless it can be helpful to inform investors about the strength and potential of the company's brand(s) to support management strategy and expected financial returns. This is more easily achieved by businesses that are dominated by or only operate under one brand.

CONCLUSION

The brand value chain is helpful in identifying, understanding, mapping, quantifying, and managing the value creation of brands. The approach identifies the key stages and how they interact to create financial results. It therefore provides an invaluable tool for managing the complex nature of brands. The value chain can be applied to all relevant brand audiences and thus extended into a comprehensive brand reputation model. The purpose of the brand value chain is to provide an economically logical framework for managing and quantifying the value creation of brands.

CHAPTER 13

RETURN ON BRAND INVESTMENT

INTRODUCTION

With brands being such important business assets that account for substantial corporate value the question of managing and measuring the investments a company makes into a brand arises. Marketing expenditures for most companies have grown exponentially over the past decade. In several industries, especially consumer goods, marketing represents more than half of total costs of goods sold (COGS). Brands as intangible assets account for between 30 percent and 80 percent of shareholder value. In most companies brands are the single most valuable asset. It is therefore not surprising that the pressure from senior management and the financial community has grown to make marketing and brand investment accountable and align their use of funds to the value-based management agenda. The days when companies accepted the view expressed by Lever Brothers founder Lord Leverhulme (among others) who reputedly said: "I know half my advertising budget is wasted. But I am not sure which half" have passed.[1] In the post-Sarbanes-Oxley world of accountability and the need to boost corporate earnings following the 2008/9 recession, management require quantifiable proof that the resources being spent on marketing can be justified to shareholders. As brand-building requires substantial investments of both time and money companies are looking for a Return on Investment (ROI) framework that optimizes resources in order to achieve maximum value creation for shareholders.

ROI – THE SHORT-TERM VIEW

Easy and close to real-time access to high frequency sales and marketing data have resulted in the development and proliferation of complex and sophisticated marketing-mix models that measure the ROI of individual marketing activities as well as optimizing the overall marketing and media budget. Based on the scanner data from the tills these models can measure the direct sales impact on marketing activities and analyze which incremental sales have been generated by which specific effort. Most of these ROI models also provide "optimal" allocation of the marketing budget across all activities to guide future spend. Some very advanced models utilize game theory to anticipate competitors' marketing activities and optimize the budget accordingly.[2] Their attraction lies in their simplicity and their base in hard data that a non-marketing professional can easily understand.

However, too much focus on short-term ROI results in reallocating funds from longer-term brand-building investments like strategic marketing and communications to short-term sales drivers like pricing and promotion. In addition, traditional media is becoming increasingly fragmented, reducing the effectiveness of mainstream media such as advertising. According to a study by the consulting firm Booz & Co. companies are shifting marketing spend from media communications (TV, radio, print) to sales-focused activities such as consumer and trade promotions. These increased their share of marketing spend by 7–8 percent during the period 2000 to 2004[3.] The study suggests that the reallocation of marketing budgets to promotions is due to the fact that their success can be easily measured. Price promotions increase sales in the short term but have a negative effect in the long term by impairing the perception of the brand. On-going price promotions and incentives lead to a downward spiral in which low prices harm brand perceptions resulting in the need for further price promotions to stabilize sales. Consumers get used to the promotion prices and the company suffers a permanent hit on its margins and the brand on its image. The incentive-based selling of US car brands has shown how such an approach harms brand perceptions and kills the margins of the business.

Brand building is a long-term process

Brand building is a long-term process that can stretch over decades as evidenced by the building of leading global brands such as Apple, BMW, Coca-Cola and Gillette. The change of brand perceptions is therefore relatively slow. The reason is that a company needs to deliver the brand to their customers through all their customer-facing activities in a constant clearly differentiated and relevant way. Due to limited capacity and interest it is a time-consuming activity to get a space in consumers' minds, particularly given the current media bombardment to which consumers are exposed. In the developed world, consumers are exposed on average to more than 3000 brand messages per day[4] Engraving a brand perception in consumers' minds does not happen quickly. Consumers need to be aware of the brand, develop knowledge of its offer, consider its relevance and difference to competing offers, and then purchase if they believe their needs are met. Obviously, given the immense choice that exists in nearly all categories, consumers cannot perform such an assessment for each brand on the market. Companies therefore need to use their resources as efficiently as possible to attract consumers' attention and loyalty. This requires a focused effort to create and deliver a distinctive and relevant brand message and delivery. Constantly and consistently strengthening and optimizing all parts of the brand value chain (see Chapter 12) enables companies to create, maintain, and grow the perception of their brands in consumers' minds. Once companies have established their brand perception it is possible to reap the economic rewards for a considerable length of time as evidenced by Coca-Cola, HP, and Kellogg's. Consumer memory tends to be durable and once information about a brand is fixed in peoples' minds it erodes very slowly.[5] Consistent brand building over time therefore creates a sustaining and accumulative effect on customers' perceptions and behaviors. The investments that companies make accumulate into a sustainable brand asset whose value can be quantified. In that respect the brand asset and investments made in the brand behave differently to physical or other intangible assets such as patents and technology. The brand asset is invested in an on-going basis through the company's actions and communications. The effect accumulates over time making each additional investment more efficient as it adds to a growing base. The effect limits are set by the relevance of the brand meeting consumer needs and financial resources.

Marketing spend creates shareholder value

Brand building creates sustainable shareholder value. According to several surveys, brands account for 30–80 percent of shareholder value, depending on the industry.[6] This supports the view that overall brand investments have a positive impact on shareholder value. The direct result of the brand's impact on shareholder value can be measured by brand value which represents the NPV of the brand's expected future earnings. Brand value is therefore a good measure of the success of brand investments. The impact on brand investments and marketing activities on brand value differ significantly. To understand these impacts it is helpful to look at each investment category separately.

The first investment category – strategic brand investments – are made periodically and provide the framework for communications and tactical investments. Strategic investments are the core brand elements, brand image advertising, product development and design, retail space as well as sales force and customer service personnel training. The core brand elements define the attributes and associations that consumers attach to the brand. They create the differentiation and relevance of the brand's offer which impacts customers' purchases and the resulting financial outcomes. Brand core elements include the brand name, core values and positioning, and some visual elements, primarily the logo. Often these core elements remain unchanged for many years or even decades as they are a big part of the reason why the company has become successful in the first place. Only strategic shifts in the sector or business require a change of these core values. Brands such as BMW, Apple, Coca-Cola, Louis Vuitton, Hermès, Nivea, Sony, Kellogg, Disney, Virgin, and IBM are just a few examples of the continuity and endurance of a brand's core elements. The Coca-Cola brand still represents refreshment, the original cola, and American heritage while the written logo, the color red, and the bottle shape are still the defining brand elements. Apple represents fun, ease of use, and style in consumer electronics represented by its iconic logo and product design. BMW still represents performance, style, and engineering quality and, although the design of the cars has changed over the years, the kidney split grill and the blue and white logo have remained core design elements. IBM is, despite a significant shift in business strategy in the 1990s, still the safe and secure IT consulting choice donning the striped logo as they have since 1972. The key effect of the core brand elements is not necessarily the beauty or aesthetics of the specific designs or symbols but the consistency and recognition they create for the brand. The Coca-Cola logo was not created by a designer but by the company's accountant in 1885. The visual core elements may, over time, be tweaked to keep them looking contemporary (e.g., 3D logos) but a major departure from the established elements needs to be well grounded in changes of business strategy and environment. Strategic repositioning of brands occurs but can be very dangerous as demonstrated by BP in Chapter 12. The creation and management of the core brand elements are relatively cheap and are made up of management workshops, consulting time, trademark registration and protection of name, logo and other elements such as colors or shapes. The ROI is very high as the majority of brand communications are directed by the core elements.

Part of the strategic core elements is the decision on how many brands are to be used and what relationship these brands have to each other. A brand that stretches across too many markets and products can quickly lose its differentiation and relevance. Some companies therefore develop specific brands for specific audiences and markets. For example, Toyota and Nissan recognized that despite their engineering and design capabilities their brands did not stretch credibly into the premium car segment. They therefore developed Lexus and Infinity brands respectively which both became successful brands albeit after a long and hard marketing push. Most car companies use a portfolio of brands to cover more markets. In many consumer good sectors the brand positioning needs to be relatively narrow to be credible and attractive to consumers. For that reason, companies in a variety of industries use a portfolio of brands that enables them to apply their competencies to a wide audience in their chosen industry. Examples are P&G and Nestlé in packaged goods, VW and BMW in cars, LVMH and PPR in fashion and luxury, and WPP and Omnicom in marketing services. The use and relationship of different brands is called brand architecture. Some companies use only one master-brand and the corporate and customer-facing brand is the same, examples are Samsung and IBM. In some cases corporate and product brand are the same but the company also uses other product brands, for example, BMW, VW, and L'Oréal. Some companies operate as pure holding companies with a portfolio of customer-facing brands such as P&G and WPP. A portfolio of brands is only wealth-creating when the net returns exceed the associated costs. In many bank or telecommunication company mergers, brands disappear because one brand takes on the role of both brands and investments are reduced accordingly. Brand architecture is therefore an important strategic brand decision. Supporting one brand is cheaper than supporting a portfolio of brands as each brand activity and investment accumulates to build the value of one brand. This is supported by academic research that has suggested that the impact of marketing variables on brand-related intangible assets may be moderated by the type of branding strategy adopted by a firm: corporate branding; house-of-brands; or mixed branding. Based on a panel data set, the results show that a master branding strategy is associated with a 58 percent higher Tobin's q value (market value/asset value) relative to a house-of-brands strategy and a 73 percent higher value than a mixed-branding strategy.[7]

The core brand elements impact on other strategic brand investments. Product development and design are often driven by the brand positioning as in the case of Apple and Samsung. Apple's product line moved from computers to MP3 players (i-Pod) and mobile phones (i-Phone) while still applying the same brand principles of fun, ease of use, and style. The Apple design style is consistent throughout its product line-up making the brand instantly recognizable. BMW is another good example in this respect. Over time the consistent application of certain design elements become core brand elements such as the grill design of BMW or Rolls-Royce. Major product developments occur in longer cycles sometimes of many years. Their impact on brand value is significant as demonstrated by brands such as Apple, Samsung, Audi, BMW, and Nintendo. Companies therefore invest significant sums in R&D. L'Oréal spends as much on R&D as it does on advertising. Samsung spends about 50 percent more on R&D than on advertising. Intel and Microsoft have some of the highest R&D budgets in the industry. These companies need new products to attract consumers to build and maintain their brands. Branded companies tend to spend more on R&D than their more commodity-based peers. A strong brand also allows for higher returns on R&D investments as the brand creates instant credibility, acceptance, and reassurance.

Core positioning also drives the image advertising and communications of the brand. For many consumer-facing businesses advertising is an essential and in many cases the most expensive component of their marketing communications. As it deals directly with the communication aspect of the brand, it can be designed to deliver brand specific messaging to influence consumers' perceptions and behaviors. This includes building awareness and knowledge of the brand, differentiation, and premium perceptions. A study by PwC claims that advertising positively affects consumers' brand perceptions and their willingness to pay a price premium for these brands. The study suggests a strong correlation between share of voice (in particular TV advertising) and consumer willingness to pay price premia. The same study stated that brand investments can shift brand preferences within 14 months.[8]

While advertising can have persistent effects on sales,[9] in most cases, the immediate sales impact is short-term with about 90 percent of the effect ceasing after 3 to 15 months.[10] Advertising contributes to building brand knowledge and attitudes.[11] Brand awareness is a function of the number of brand exposures and experiences accumulated by consumers.[12]

While the specific effect of advertising on consumer perceptions and experiences depends on a wide range of factors including message content, media scheduling, product category, and competitive activities,[13] overall higher advertising spend tends to positively affect brand attitudes and perceptions.[14] The effect of advertising on consumer brand perception can be sustaining and accumulative[15] as each brand message and touch point builds and reinforces other brand messages and touch points improving the effectiveness of each additional message and exposure.[16] The image communication of the brand is accumulative and each advertising campaign consistent with the core positioning builds the brand perceptions in consumers' minds. Brand advertising builds awareness, knowledge, and preference. While most companies still spend the majority of their advertising budget on TV advertising there has been a shift towards direct mail and the Internet because the direct impact of these media on sales is relatively easy to measure. In many companies, advertising is one of the largest marketing expenses.[17]

Another strategic brand investment is retail space such as shops and dealerships. They are main brand touch points and ultimately the point of sale. Not all businesses can afford to control their point of sale but the ones that do make substantial investments in their retail outlets. Most leading luxury brands have reduced their concessions and focused on their owned retail space. In 2003, Prada paid US$87 million for its flagship store in Tokyo, which was the largest single investment made by an italian company in Japan since World War II.[18] Brands like Gucci, Hermès, BMW, Apple, and McDonald's invest enormous amounts in their retail outlets. The returns are high, with Apple now selling about 15 percent of its products through its own branded stores. Many brands (Samsung, Sony, Nike, Adidas) have established, at a minimum, flagship stores to showcase their products in a brand-controlled environment and for Starbucks the retail environment is one of the core drivers of brand value. Increasingly, the web presence has become, for many brands, an important retail space albeit at significantly lower costs then their physical counterparts. The retail spaces form a crucial part of the brand experience and their design is guided by the core brand elements.

For service brands and brands that have significant control over their retail outlets customer service and sales personnel are key in delivering the brand experience. Staff behavior needs to follow brand-influenced rules and guidelines. The behavior of the customer-facing personnel is a key influencing factor on customers' purchase decisions. The experience in an Apple or Louis Vuitton shop will reflect the different nature of the brands. The additional brand-specific investments beyond salaries and compensations are relatively low but the return is substantial. For a brand like Starbucks the staff behavior is a core driver of brand value.

Sponsorships are also strategic brand investments that can build sustainable brand value. At the lowest level they create awareness due to the exposure of the brand logo and provide hospitality opportunities for high-end clients and multipliers. Their deeper brand building occurs only if the sponsorship is properly activated through appropriate brand image advertising support. Nike, Samsung, and Accenture have made efficient use of their sponsorship investments. The investment amounts can be substantial. Samsung Electronics spends about US$100 million on their Olympic sponsorship including activation, and Accenture has spent about US$65 million per year on its Tiger Woods sponsorship.[19] For Accenture, the sponsorship has become a key vehicle for its brand communications.

Promotions are tactical marketing activities that can build the brand in situations where the brand moves into new markets or needs to revitalize itself. Consumer perception-building promotions communicate distinctive brand attributes and contribute to the development and reinforcement of the brand image.[20] On an aggregate level, companies are spending more on promotional activities than on advertising with about 60–75 percent of promotional budgets being spent on sales promotion.[21] The impact on promotions, however, differs between brand perception building initiatives and pure price promotions. Consumer promotions, such as samples, tempt trial and can assist in shifting consumer perceptions by exposing more potential customers to the brand experience. Short-term financial promotions can help in product introductions and accelerating trial sales in the short term. However, over-use and reliance on financial promotions can destroy brand value on a large scale. The downfall of the US car brands is an example of how a strategic focus on short-term sales push through financial incentives has ruined brand perception and led to the long term decline of brands such as Chrysler, Chevrolet, and Ford. Price promotions destroy brand value as well as companies' profit margins.

An academic research study assessed the impact of brand investments on brand value based on the Best Global brands study published annually in *BusinessWeek*.[22] It assessed the impact and optimal levels of key brand investments such as R&D, advertising, and promotional spend on brand value creation. According to the research, the return on R&D spending increases for expenses below US$200 million and reaches saturation point around US$1 billion, beyond which it does not significantly increase brand value. This is supported by industry experience from companies with large R&D budgets, such as Microsoft and Philips.[23] It is also in line with the flat maximum principle[24] that states that large changes in spending do not generate big changes in profits.

The positive impact of advertising expenditure on a company's stock market performance has consistently been proven most recently in the example of Samsung.[25] Marketing expenses also create a significant barrier to market entry, as the high amount of spend required to change consumer perception deters potential competitors from entering a marketing-intensive environment.[26] Advertising can directly influence sales, market share, and relative price.[27] Advertising contributes most effectively to brand value in a spending range between US$200 million and US$4.6 billion.

A further study suggests that only large-scale promotions have an impact on brand value, while an investment volume below US$2 billion appears to have little impact. This is not surprising as promotions work mainly as a direct sales impetus that needs scale to be effective.[28]

A study separating the long-term effects of marketing on an increase in sales volume and sales value concluded that most of the increase in volume is due to advertising and discounting, and most of the variation in value is due to distribution and product.[29]

Summary

There is sufficient evidence to prove that marketing investments have a positive impact on brand value and shareholder value. The value creation is accumulative and sustainable. It materializes in the long term and their effect is therefore not appropriately captured by short-term ROI measures. The proliferation and easy access of scanner and sales data has led to a disproportionate shift towards short-term marketing activities in particular, sales promotions. Sales promotions are the one activity which only creates value if used sparsely and supports the overall brand image. Continual or frequent sales promotions destroy brand value and profit margins. The most effective mix of different marketing activities depends on their brand-building potential. For that reason an ROI approach is required that assesses the long-term brand value creation of each activity and their optimal interplay to achieve the highest return on brand investments.

NEED FOR A LONG-TERM VIEW

While marketing ROI and mix models have provided useful tools for quantifying the short-term effect of specific initiatives they have also focused marketing accountability on the short-term. Brand building, however, is a long-term process stretching over several years and requires long-term commitment and vision. With brand assets accounting now for a substantial part of corporate wealth, an ROI approach is needed that reflects the nature of the value creation of the asset.[30]

No company would use scanner data and changes in short-term sales to assess the return on capital expenditures. The accounting depreciation of many fixed assets such as land and buildings stretches up to 20 years. About 70 percent of the leading 100 global brands are older than 50 years outlasting the life span of the average US corporation and the useful economic life of nearly all other business assets. According to all leading accounting standards acquired brands need to be capitalized on the balance sheet and amortized according to their useful economic life which can be 20 years or more. Brands with an infinite economic use remain a capitalized asset and their value is adjusted downwards (see Chapter 10) according to annual impairment test. Given the fact that on average more than 70 percent of a company's share price is based on expected cash flows beyond 3 years, and that about 25 years of future cash flow expectations make up about three-fourths of the NPV of most companies, the long-term value of the brand as one of the company's most important assets should be managed according to its expected long-term value generation.[31] This requires looking at the brand as a long-term asset that needs long-term planning and investment. A suitable ROI model therefore needs to address the short- and long-term impact of marketing activities.

ROI calculation

In business and financial analysis, ROI is used as a performance measure to assess the efficiency of an investment or to compare the efficiency of a number of different investments. Calculation of ROI is relatively easy, the benefit or return of an investment is divided by its costs. To make the investment worthwhile the benefit has to exceed its costs. The result is expressed as a percentage or a ratio that assesses the investment. The return on investment formula is simple:

ROI = Net Return/Investment

If an investment has a negative ROI, or if there are other opportunities with a higher ROI, then the investment should be not be undertaken.

ROI is a very simple and versatile tool as it can be applied to nearly all investment decisions. The resulting ratio provides a clear and easily understood result. The difficulty with ROI lies in the definition of its two components: return and investment. For example, a marketer may compare two different brands by dividing the revenue that each brand has generated by its respective marketing expenses. A financial analyst, however, may compare the same two brands by dividing the net income of each brand by the total value of all resources that have been employed to make and sell the brands. Thus the ROI can be positive for the marketer but negative for the financial analyst. Understanding the inputs is therefore crucial in assessing ROI. This becomes even more complex and controversial when assessing ROI for specific functions and departments such as marketing or R&D.

Brand ROI

Return on brand or marketing investment is defined as the relationship between the spend on and investments in the brand and the economic return they create. Brand ROI is a metric for optimizing marketing spend for the short and long term by comparing brand specific economic returns and investments. An improved brand ROI will lead to increased revenues and profits for the same amount of spend. The assessment is complicated by the time impact of marketing investments and initiatives. Some brand initiatives such as direct mail campaigns focus on short-term sales increase and value creation. Others, such as improved customer experience or brand image campaigns, show their effect on value creation over several years. The short-term ROI assessment is most widely used because it creates an easily measurable link between investment and return, due to the short measurement period.

For example, if a company spends US$1 million on a short-term initiative that results in incremental brand earnings of US$250,000 then the ROI (the amount of incremental brand earnings for each dollar of marketing spend) is 25 percent. This calculation works if incremental sales and earnings can be properly identified. This entails ensuring that during the period of the campaign no other marketing activities or unexpected events could have caused the increase in revenues. If parallel to the campaign other activities occur separating incremental sales becomes more difficult. This short-term assessment is relatively simple and easily executed. For short-term investments a simple determination of revenue and Brand Earnings per dollar spent for each marketing activity can suffice to make decisions on improving the entire marketing mix. However, strategic brand investments often show their effect with a delay and over a longer period of time, sometimes many years. Such marketing investments include changes in brand positioning, product design, sponsorships, or customer touch points such as customer service, sales staff training, and retail design. Measuring the return on these investments requires assessing their impact over many years. One way many companies tackle the issue is to use brand value as the asset value that relates to the brand or marketing investment. For example, if the value of the brand before the investment amounts to US$1 billion and the company invests in a five-year sponsorship deal with an annual investment of US$20 million the incremental brand value generated by the initiative over the period needs to exceed US$100 million to make the investment worthwhile. If the value of the brand increased to US$1.12 billion and no other additional investments or initiatives were taken then the return of the sponsorship was 120 percent. The additional US$120 million represent the additional NPV of brand cash flows generated by the US$100 million sponsorship investment. The brand value includes the impact of the sponsorship investment on customer perceptions, behaviors, and financial impact (see Chapters 5 and 12).

The starting point for brand ROI is brand value and a detailed understanding of the brand value chain, i.e. the link between customer perceptions, behaviors, and their financial impact in the form of revenues and profits. The historical analysis should ideally cover at least a period of 3 years. Longer time frames can be used if there is sufficient data available and there is no change in the underlying market conditions and consumer sentiment. In times of economic crisis and structural change in the economic landscape, as encountered in 2008/9, an analysis of previous crises in different markets can be very helpful. The historical analyses then need to be blended with forward looking information and data such as GDP growth, disposable income, shopping priorities, and consumer sentiment. These analyses will provide trend lines for sales and profits that can be extrapolated forward. Such an exercise will require the collaboration of marketing, planning, and financial professionals. The data quality is important and it may require the purchase of additional market and research data. A variety of statistical modeling tools can be used and can include: econometrics; choice modeling; multivariate random forecasting; and structural equation modeling.

Ultimately, the purpose of these tools is to identify any cause-and-effect relationships between inputs used to build the brand and their economic outcome. Due to the wide range of factors and variables involved, this is a data-intensive exercise. It is important not to get drawn into impenetrable black box modeling tools that cannot be understood without a PhD in mathematics as this delegates the decision process to some "experts" with the potential exclusion of sufficient checks and balances. The logic and results, as well as the limits of these models, need to be understood by marketing and financial professionals to avoid reliance on the "black box." Ultimately, all these models have severe limits and should be used as tools and not blindly and mechanically relied upon. A well constructed and understood cause-and-effect model can be a very useful tool for guiding brand-and business-related investment decisions. However, depending on the data a simplified framework may be more appropriate for short-term management. For example, based on an in-depth brand value assessment specific brand perception drivers can be identified such as certain associations and attitudes and used for short-term performance and success metrics on a monthly or quarterly basis assuming the appropriate data are tracked for these time-frames. The strategic brand value drivers can be reassessed or adjusted according to the annual valuation of the brand. The annual ROI calculation is then adjusted based on actual perception metrics as well as behavioral impact and financial delivery i.e. brand earnings and value.

The brand ROI approach (incremental brand value/brand investment) captures the short-and long-term value creation of brand investments by linking brand specific spending and initiatives to their impact on consumer perceptions, behaviors, and related financial outcomes. An important aspect is the identification and definition of brand investments. There is a tendency to focus or limit brand investments to the traditional marketing communications, in particular, advertising and promotions. While these are key platforms for communicating the brand message, other brand-driven investments can have an equal or even greater impact on value creation. Strategic brand investments such as product development and design can have a large and long lasting impact on brand perception and delivery. Leading multinational companies such as Samsung Electronics, BMW, and Intercontinental Hotels Group use their brand to guide a wide range of customer-facing touch points including product design and development, point of sale and retail design as well as sales force and personnel training. These tend to be more strategic and relatively less frequent than advertising and other communications.

Once the relationships between specific brand drivers and their economic impact have been identified and quantified, the framework can be used to model and assess the likely success of different brand investments. Based on statistical analyses, the financial value the brand contributes, compared to other value drivers such as distribution, pricing, services, and other factors, can be identified.

This is a sophisticated metric that balances marketing and business analyses and is used increasingly by many of the world's leading organizations to measure the economic (that is, cash-flow derived) benefits created by marketing investments. This approach offers a way to prioritize investments and allocate marketing and other resources on a scientific basis. It is, however, intensively data driven and requires sophisticated cause-and-effect modeling tools to link changes in consumer attitudes to changes in their behavior. It also requires deep and rich data sets. However, with modern research techniques and statistical modeling tools, such an approach can be implemented at little or no additional costs if current market research budgets are consolidated and optimized.

Brand ROI is an advanced metric tool used by a number of forward-thinking firms interested in value-based brand management and aligning the assessment of brand investments with all the investments of the company. Based on the brand value chain and the cause-and-effect modeling results, brand investments are determined, this includes decisions about how much money to spend on the advertising for each brand, product, market, or target group. Once the initiatives have been implemented they need to be constantly checked through actual changes in financial and marketing parameters to see if they are working.

By using the brand ROI framework, companies can prioritize and optimize their brand investments to increase their brand value. A very successful example is Samsung Electronics that, at the beginning of its turnaround at the end of the 1990s, set ambitious brand value targets and established sophisticated brand analytics to understand and implement strategic and tactical brand investments. Samsung used extensive data on market variables, brand share, marketing expenses, and other variables. It ran simulations to understand how and where marketing investments yielded the highest returns. For example, this led Samsung to their Olympic sponsorship, a reassessment of distribution channels, and a focus on TV advertising in the US in the last 6 months of the year (the main sales season for consumer electronics).[32]

ESTABLISHING A BRAND ROI FRAMEWORK

First, the key elements that influence the brand's value creation from a customer's perspective need to be identified and defined. These elements then need to be integrated into a brand value chain that links the brand with financial value creation derived from customers' purchases. Through a detailed cause and affect analysis and modeling exercise the relationship between brand values, perceptions, touch points and their impact on customer behavior, and the related financial outcomes can be determined and quantified. The pinnacle of this relationship is the value of the brand which breaks down in its components and linkages (the brand value chain). This knowledge emerges from market research or in-market experimentation that shows how existing and prospective customers make choices in a competitive marketplace.

Each customer touch point is analyzed and assessed according to its contribution to value creation in the context of the other touch points. This exercise identifies and quantifies the elements that impact customer demand and loyalty.

Segmentation

It is also necessary to prioritize efforts according to their value creation potential. This means a clear understanding and definition of the target markets. Most brands have several circles of customers ranging from the committed loyalist who will only buy the particular, to opportunistic or occasional customers who consider that brand alongside others and buy it depending on price and convenience. In addition, there are potential customers to whom the brand could be relevant but who are not currently buying the brand. In assessing brand ROI it is important to understand the return options for each customer segment. A price promotion may attract new customers but an improvement in customer service may reduce customer loss. In many sectors customer acquisition costs outstrip the costs of retaining customers. A price promotion provides a short-term increase in revenues whereas the improved customer service secures cash flows from a long-term customer relationship. Customer lifetime value is a useful way of balancing such investments. This is also true when assigning investments in different geographic markets. Investments in countries where the brand is little known but with substantial value potential may require longer-term investments than in established markets. A well-known technology brand used to allocate its brand investments as a percentage of revenues and as a result spending focused heavily on established markets such as US and Europe. This changed once the company had assessed the value of its brands on a global scale revealing the brand value opportunities in some large emerging markets. Based on the brand valuation, the company switched to a brand ROI approach that aligned marketing spending with actual value creation. Since then the return on its marketing investments has nearly doubled.

Touch points

To optimize the allocation of marketing resources it is mandatory to identify, understand, and quantify the impact of the brand's customer touch points. Touch points are all elements that connect the company and the consumer. Key customer touch points are the product or service offer, price, point of sale presence, customer service, packaging, the Internet, sales representatives and shop assistants, media communications including advertising, sponsorships, corporate identity, PR, direct mail, and trade and price promotions. Depending on the brand's industry and business model some of these touch points will be more relevant or controllable. For example, many services and luxury goods businesses control a significant number or all of their distribution outlets or sales force. They can therefore, directly influence the customer even at the point of sale. Most packaged goods and consumer electronics brands, on the other hand, sell entirely through third parties such as retailers or intermediaries thus having rather less control over the point of sale. At the same time, their products are placed next to, or near, competing offers. They can influence their point of sale through shelf management, retailer sales force training, and education. If they own a strong brand portfolio, such as P&G and Nestlé, they can force weaker brands off the shelf through packaged deals. However, in the end it is consumer pull and the shelf turnover that decides how long retailers are willing to stock a brand. Retail space is so valuable that weak brands disappear relatively quickly. The focus on such brands is therefore on product innovation, packaging, advertising, and price. The ROI framework allows allocation of marketing funds between touch points and optimizes their investments from an overall budget impact perspective. For example, Samsung Electronics' product design and development as well as channel marketing have been key touch points invested in by the company to achieve its outstanding growth in brand value over a relatively short period of time. Starbucks' success has been mainly the result of its store design and employee training – advertising has only commenced recently.

Implementing brand ROI metrics

The brand ROI analysis also helps to optimize the communication of core values by assessing which mix of values and attributes has the strongest impact on perceptions and behaviors. Messaging content can be aligned with touch points and attributes can be turned up and down to achieve the most economically effective impact. For example, a sports sponsorship can focus on communicating performance as a value while local corporate social responsibility (CSR) efforts can be focused on communicating "togetherness" and care. This means that brand ROI can also guide messaging and content focus at each key touch point. To make ROI a useful management tool for enhancing the value of the brand short- and long-term metrics need to be considered and used.

While brand building is a long-term affair, most companies will have already established a certain level of brand value. That value represents the cumulative result of the company's total brand-building activities. The brand ROI framework is derived from the brand valuation method and the brand value chain. It needs to measure short- and long-term impact of brand and marketing investments. There needs to be a balance between the short- and long-term performances of the brand. If the short-term bias is too strong, investments are focused on short-term sales enhancing activities such as price promotions that will harm the perception and long-term value creation of the brand. If the long-term bias is too strong investments can shift towards hypothetical returns that never actually materialize. Both short- and long-term metrics are required to optimize brand investments.

Short-term metrics measure the relatively immediate impact of all marketing investments. These include maintenance investments to ensure that the value of the brand does not decline and growth investments to increase the value of the brand. While all companies will want to increase the value of their brand, budget constraints and diminishing returns will limit the investment possibilities. For example, a company may be able to reduce investments in one market or product group in order to take advantage of the opportunities in another market. It is also heavily dependent on competitors' activities.

For a brand-appropriate ROI approach, perception and behavioral data need to be measured and linked as perceptions are lead indicators while behavior tends to lag. Ultimately, brand investments need to deliver financial results. That does not mean every activity will yield instant results. It can take years to communicate a new brand message before it creates economic value. However, if after 18 months no positive impact can be detected the messaging needs to be scrutinized and if necessary abandoned. Most of the available marketing-mix models and pricing and promotion analysis tools measure the short-term impact (1 to 3 months) of marketing activities on sales. This is helpful to fine-tune tactical marketing activities to improve the short-term performance of the brand. Promotional tactics, in particular, are easily countered by competition so their effects are usually short-lived. Apart from the short-term sales impact, some marketing activities also have a long-term impact. There are two types of long-term brand investments. The first type are strategic investments such as positioning, corporate identity, brand advertising campaigns, Internet presence, product development and design, and shop design that are made at less frequent intervals and set the scene for other brand investments. Some of these strategic investments last a very long time and only require periodic adjustment. The positioning and corporate identity of a brand can remain unchanged for many years. Some even remain with little adjustment for decades. The positioning and identity of the BMW brand has been consistent since the 1990s. The core positioning of the Coca-Cola brand stems from the 1970s. The second type of long-term brand investments are cumulative brand investments such as advertising that build brand value through frequency of use. The more consumers are exposed to brand messaging the better their knowledge about the brand will become.

While measuring short-term sales impact is relatively easy, assessing long-term brand impact is much more difficult. It requires the ability to understand, identify, and quantify cause and affect relationships between marketing activities, consumer perceptions, consumer behavior, and financial outcomes. This requires the collection and modeling of a complex set of marketing and financial data. The quality of the analysis is dependent on the quality of the questionnaire and the survey sample which needs to be representative of buyers in the specific category/industry being analyzed. Using actual consumer behavior rather than their responses to a survey questionnaire has the advantage of eliminating biases from responses that do not accurately reflect consumers brand perceptions, but the disadvantage is that it limits the responses observed to brands and products purchased even though the consumer may have awareness and perceptions about brands they have not purchased. It is therefore best to use a combination of both approaches. There is also the issue of the model quality, accuracy, and predictability. There is a difference between parallel moving metrics measured through correlating the respective data and causal relationships that can measure cause and effect. Advanced statistical analyses such as structural equation and least squares modeling techniques can deliver impressive results in identifying and predicting causal relationships. These techniques can be used to model the brand value chain and derive predictive outcomes.

Once the brand value chain has been established and the financial value of the brand calculated, key metrics can be identified for use in an on-going measurement of the impact and return on brand investments. If the brand value chain model is established and in place then new marketing data can be integrated into the ROI model to assess the effectiveness of brand investments. ROI can be assessed on an aggregate level of brand value as well as on single components and their interaction with the brand value. The individual components can be integrated into a scorecard for managing brand investments and activities.

Some of the key metrics are as follows:

- *Brand awareness*: This measures whether consumers are aware of the brand and if so, at what level. Aided awareness measures whether consumers connect the brand with the category when the name is mentioned. If aided awareness is low then the brand has not penetrated consumers' minds. Unaided awareness shows that consumers associate the brand without being prompted with the category. Top of mind measures whether the brand is the first the consumers think of in the specific category. It demonstrates a strong presence of the brand in consumers' minds.
- *Brand knowledge*: This metric measures the extent of the consumers' knowledge about the brand beyond the name. The greater the brand knowledge the better consumers can assess the brand's offer.
- *Brand attributes and association*: This measures the attributes consumers associate with the brand and how the brand performs on each attribute relative to its competitors. They represent the functional (e.g., quality) and emotional (e.g., status, image) utility the brand provides. In order to be effective a brand needs to represent a unique mix of attributes and associations that differentiate the brand from competitors and make its offers relevant to consumers.
- *Differentiation*: This is derived from the performance on brand attributes and associations. Differentiation ensures that the brand stands out from its competitors.
- *Relevance*: In order to be considered, a brand needs to provide a relevant offer that meets consumer need. Price or very specific brand elements can limit consumer relevance.
- *Consideration*: This is the first step in a potential purchase. Here the brand is seriously considered as purchase option.
- *Preference*: Being the desired choice indicates a clear preference and likelihood of purchase. There need to be significant reasons for non-purchase which tend to be price and financially based.
- *Choice*: The brand is the consumer's choice and his/her intended purchase
- *Satisfaction*: This metric only refers to customers who have previous purchasing experience of the brand. Customer satisfaction is

better in measuring functional or material attributes than emotional factors.

- *Advocacy*: This measures the likelihood of the consumer recommending the brand to others. Advocacy is key in driving "word of mouth" advertising. This is one of the most powerful purchase drivers as it usually comes from credible and trusted parties such as family, friends, colleagues, or specialized agencies such as JD Power, Which, or Stiftung Warentest.
- *Loyalty*: This is an important metric for sustainability of brand value. The more loyal the customer base is the more predictable the brand's cash flow will be. In addition, brands that have a very loyal customer base need to spend less on customer acquisition which in many service businesses is a large cost factor.
- *Sales price*: Price is an indication of the appreciation of the brand relative to its competitors and creates direct value at it is a key component of the companies' revenues. An increase in price directly increases profit margins but only if the net results exceed potential drops in volume and frequency.
- *Sales volume*: This is an indication about the relevance of the offer. Sales volume also contributes to revenues and works in tandem with price.
- *Sales frequency*: This is another indicator of relevance and also contributes directly to revenues.
- *Intangible earnings*: These are the earnings entirely attributable to the intangibles of the business. They are calculated by deducting the brand operating costs, a return for the capital employed, and tax payments from the revenues that are generated. Intangible earnings are similar to concepts such as EVA and economic profit.
- *Brand impact*: This metric measures the impact the brand has on customer choice relative to other intangibles. Brand impact is measured for each purchase driver and aggregated to an overall percentage representing the impact of the brand on revenues and profit generation.
- *Brand earnings*: This number represents the earnings generated by the brand. It is calculated by multiplying the brand impact percentage with intangible earnings.
- *Brand value*: This metric look at the overall value creation of the brand within the company's business context. Brand value is calculated as the NPV of the future expected brand earnings discounted with the weighted average cost of capital (WACC).

The use of the brand valuation framework for ROI calculations depends on the availability and frequency of the reporting of the above data. Many research and financial data are available on a monthly basis. Once the value of the brand has been calculated it can easily be updated depending on the internal data flow and availability. Some companies update their brand value as an on-going process while other companies value their brands on a quarterly or annual basis making it part of the overall business review. Most companies will already collect the data that are necessary to calculate brand value and ROI. If this is not the case then these frameworks can help companies adjust and redirect their research budgets toward the brand value framework. Brand value is at the core of ROI as it represents the brand's contribution to the underlying business. Brand-building activities need to be assessed according to their value creation which means brand and subsequently shareholder value. Each initiative and investments needs to create economic value. The brand ROI calculation is therefore:

Brand ROI = Incremental brand value/Brand investment

As brand value represents the NPV of all expected brand earnings marketing activities need to enhance brand value over and above their cost and the cost of capital or WACC. That means the expected incremental NPV of the respective activity needs to be larger than its cost. The brand ROI approach aligns the assessment of brand investments with that of other company assets, and puts marketing expenses on par with other investments such as capital expenditures. The ROI approach treats the brand as an asset that needs to be maintained and built according to the same principle as other business assets.

Measuring brand ROI requires a balance between short- and long-term metrics. Short-term metrics ensure that marketing activities impact consumers' behaviors and create financial value. This can be achieved through the on-going analysis of sales data provided by scanners or other sources. At the same time, the other metrics identified earlier need to be monitored to ensure that strategic long-term brand investments can be implemented and that short-term initiatives do not undermine brand perceptions, e.g., price promotions. In order to ensure that marketing activities deliver value companies need to classify investments according to their goal and impact. Price promotions will show immediate sales uplift but, if they become the focus of marketing investments they will destroy brand value in the long term. This will be picked up in the brand perception research. On the other hand, a strategic marketing initiative needs not only to influence perceptions but also behaviors and their financial results. The brand ROI framework and metrics allow for such a balance. It is also important not to limit brand investments to traditional marketing communications such as advertising, promotions, web presence, corporate identity, and PR. Product development and design, pricing strategy, point of sale presence, channel marketing, sales, and customer service personnel training can be equally important. In fact for many brands they are more important than traditional communications. One of the most effective brand-building investments for Samsung and Apple were product development and design as well as channel marketing. Apple has heavily invested in its own distribution which now accounts for more than 20 percent of its revenues. The retail investments of luxury brands such as Louis Vuitton, Prada, and Gucci substantially outstrip their media investments. The brand ROI can differ significantly by initiative. Companies therefore need to measure ROI in the short- and long-term.

CONCLUSION

Most marketing investments create brand and shareholder value. They are cumulative and sustainable, building on a company's most valuable assets. As such, marketing expenditures should not be only measured by their immediate impact on sales but on their creation of sustainable brand and shareholder value. The availability of, and easy access to, sales data from store scanners and the Internet has led companies to shift marketing expenses to short-term activities such as sales promotions, direct mail, and the Internet as their success is easily measured against clear financial results. However, short-term marketing activities as a strategy can destroy brand value and ultimately shareholder value. To capture the long-term value creation of brand investments, companies need to employ sophisticated cause-and-effect models that can measure and optimize the impact of each activity on customer perceptions, behaviors, and their financial impact. Only then can a meaningful return on investment be assessed and calculated. Although complex, such models should not rely on impenetrable black box approaches with questionable correlations but on sound business models that link perception to value creation. A brand ROI approach based on the economic value of the brand and the brand value chain provides a framework for assessing and managing short- and long-term investments in brand assets. After all efficient brand-building is part of a company's responsibility to the shareholders who provide the financial means. Brand ROI is a framework that, with the right data input, can be sufficiently robust and representative to measure the impact of marketing investments on brand performance and sustainability. The alternative would be to remain at the short-term level and sacrifice brand and shareholder value.

CHAPTER 14

BRANDS AND THE STOCK MARKET

Brands are key corporate assets accounting for a significant portion of shareholder value. In 1987, the price to tangible book value of the Standard & Poor's 500 Stock Index (S&P 500) exceeded 2 indicating that intangible assets were starting to become more valuable than the asset base reported on companies' books. This ratio peaked at around 7 during the dotcom frenzy and stabilized after the 2008/9 market crash at 2.7 as of the end of the first half of 2009. The average price to tangible book value of the S&P 500 between 1985 and 2009 is 3.9 indicating that about 74 percent of the average long-term stock market value of all companies (including utilities, real estate, commodity and manufacturing businesses) included in the S&P 500 is generated by intangible assets such as brands, customer base, patents, organizational frameworks, and channel relationships. This is remarkable as the share price represents the NPV of all of the companies' future expected cash flows.

Many financial valuation studies and text books show that expectations of future performance are the main driver of shareholder returns. Across industries and stock exchanges, about 70–80 percent of a company's market value can be explained only by cash flow expectations beyond the next 3 years. Brand specific studies also revealed that companies with strong brands consistently generate higher total returns to shareholders than their industry counterparts[1]. These companies have proven their ability to generate superior returns in the past and their brands can convince investors that they will be able continue delivering these returns in the future. Studies conducted by consulting firms PwC, Interbrand, Millward Brown, and others demonstrate that brands account for 30–80 percent of shareholder value.[2] Over and above the past performance companies with strong brands generate higher expectations of future performance as a powerful brand is more likely to attract and retain consumers/customers in the future, can be leveraged into new channels, geographies, and businesses as Apple, Disney, McDonalds, IBM, and others have demonstrated.

Investor's assessment of a company's future expected performance is represented by the price/earnings (P/E), i.e. the share price divided by annual earnings to shareholders. In general, a high P/E suggests that investors are expecting higher earnings growth in the future compared to companies with a lower P/E. Companies that are expected to exist for longer and/or grow their earnings faster attract higher P/E ratios and have higher share prices. Although without further background on the underlying company and its markets, P/E ratios can easily result in a misleading interpretation, they are a key assessment ratio of the investment community. For the past 5 years the owner of one of the world's most valuable brands, The Coca-Cola Company, was trading on an average P/E ratio of 21. Coca-Cola is the world's largest beverage company and produces a range of non-alcoholic beverages including leading global brands such as Sprite, Fanta, and most notably Coca-Cola and Diet Coke. These four brands are among the world's top five non-alcoholic sparkling beverage brands. Although Coca-Cola is an excellent company it is not operating in high-growth markets. Consumption of carbonated drinks is in a slow decline and more than half of its revenues and profits are generated in mature developed markets (56 percent of net revenues[3]). Nevertheless, as indicated by the 5 years average P/E ratio of 21, investors continuously believe that the company can deliver about 20 years' worth of earnings (considering the discounted future earnings). Despite the rise of own label offers from retailers and squeezed consumers around the world investors believe that Coca-Cola's brands, its management, and other assets can deliver more than two decades' worth of further profits. This is an example of investors' faith in the ability of companies with strong brands, like Coca-Cola, to generate profits more or less into perpetuity. Not surprisingly, Warren Buffet's Berkshire Hathaway owns more than 8% of the shares of The Coca-Cola Company, making it its largest shareholder.

In assessing the share price of a company analysts and investors are looking at a firm's potential and capability to grow and deliver its profits in the future. There are three main drivers of profit growth: revenues; profit margins; and capital efficiency. Investors are looking for companies to deliver revenue and profit growth simultaneously. P/E ratios are positively correlated with organic revenue growth suggesting that top-line growth is rewarded by higher share prices.[4] This is exactly what strong brands can deliver. There is now substantial research evidence

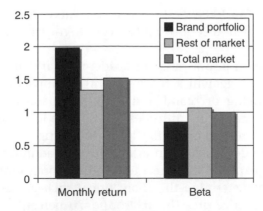

FIGURE 14.1 **Performance of brand portfolio**
Source: see Madden, Fehle and Fournier (2006).

suggesting that strong brands correlate with superior share price performance. Aaker and Jacobson used a market research database called EquiTrend to examine the extent to which consumers' quality perception of a brand provides information about a firm's stock returns. Based on a panel data set of 34 publicly traded firms between 1991 and 1993, Aaker and Jacobson found a statistically significant positive relationship between quality perception and stock returns.[5] Research based on brand values published by Interbrand in different rankings including the *Financial Times* and *BusinessWeek* until 2006 has indicated that strong brands not only deliver greater stock returns than a relevant benchmark portfolio but also do so with lower risk.[6] The survey compared a portfolio of US quoted companies which brands are included in the survey (brand portfolio) with the rest of US stocks (rest of market) and the overall US market (see Figure 14.1).

Although different portfolio strategies i.e., the weighting of companies' stocks owning the brands, produce different results the study shows that the brand portfolio outperforms the overall market as well as the rest of market portfolios with respect to return and risk. The brand portfolio outperformed the non-brand portfolio by about 48 percent and the total market by 30 percent in average monthly performance with a beta of 0.85. It suggests that brand value provides an additional explanation to shareholder value and that companies that own strong brands listed in the *BusinessWeek* survey have superior risk-adjusted performance. Similar evidence is provided by Millward Brown that found that the return of a portfolio made up of companies included in their BrandZ Top 100 over the 3 years the survey has been published delivered in the period 2006–8 a 20 percent higher return than the S&P 500 index.[7]

There have been also a range of academic marketing studies looking at brand management activities and their impact on share prices including changing of brand and corporate names,[8] new product introductions,[9] and brand attitudes.[10] Also, the links between advertising and brand-related intangible assets including perceived quality[11] and brand attitude[12] have been established. In addition, there is also research that quantifies the direct and indirect brand influence on all the factors that determine the share price, such as cash flow, earnings, and share price growth, at around 70 percent.[13] The breadth of the above studies clearly supports the notion that strong brands significantly enhance share prices and that improvements in brand perceptions have a significant and positive impact on firm valuation.[14]

Although putting brands on the balance sheet was a big issue for accountants and consultants it has had little impact on investor perceptions and how analysts assess the value of share prices. This is due to a focus on expected future cash flows rather than changes in the accounting regime. Analysts and investors can be influenced by changes in brand investments and initiatives but tend to be most affected by their financial impact. Changes in share prices are driven by expectations and changes in a company's financial performance in particular by growth in EBITDA, cash flow and earnings per share (EPS). The better the growth prospects for revenues and profits the higher investors will value the stock. If the company can grow revenues and profits at a faster rate than its tangible assets it creates more intangible and brand value. However, financial results are lagging indicators. The effect of the brand happens earlier when they impact consumers' minds and purchasing behaviors. Stock analysts try to pick up all available information on the companies they cover ranging from market research data to brand and business rankings. In addition, companies host analyst presentations and discussions in which directions about future investments and expected results are either explained or can be interpreted for use.

However, brand specific information reported by their corporate owners is very scarce. Even with consumer goods companies where brands account for around 80 percent of value, the disclosure of brand investments and performance is close to non-existent. The Coca-Cola Company provides little information about one of its largest assets, the Coca-Cola brand, which according to the *BusinessWeek*'s annual brand survey is estimated to be worth around US$68 billion[15] or around 50 percent of the company's market capitalization. The company is proud to claim that the Coca-Cola brand is the most valuable brand in the survey. Yet, there is little of information on the performance of this asset and how it is maintained and invested in. Even the reporting on the acquired brands capitalized on the balance sheet is thin. The 2008 financial statements report US$4 billion of capitalized trademarks and advertising expenses of US$2.9 billion. In the notes there is some explanation on the names of the brands that have been capitalized. However, compared to the detailed reporting and explanations on capital expenditures, tangible assets such as property, plant and equipment, and the financial hedging strategy, the information on the brand assets is minimal. Although this is partly a result of the oddities of the accounting regulations the lack of disclosure or information about the performance and investments made in the companies most valuable assets, such as the brands, is remarkable. This situation is not limited to The Coca-Cola Company. Other consumer-facing businesses such as McDonald's, Apple, Disney, Sony, BMW, Nokia, LVMH, and Inditex do not report significantly more on the performance on their brands. Although there have been many companies such as Samsung, HP, The Coca-Cola Company, Philips, and others that have been happy to report that they own valuable brands that are ranked in the *BusinessWeek*'s Best Global Brands survey further detail on their brand is scarce.

This is probably a function of limited interest by investors and analysts and little desire of management to disclose competitive information. Financial analysts focus on the analysis and modeling of financial and economic data to assess the value of the entire business to derive their share price recommendations. Although information on marketing initiatives and brand performance is of interest most financial analysts feel much more comfortable with financial data as this is the framework they have been trained in and it is also the language of capital markets. Most analysts look with interest at the brand value surveys published by different consulting firms but they either have a limited understanding about how they have been put together or question the validity of the results. A survey among financial analysts in London showed that there was limited demand for more detailed disclosure on marketing assets and investments.[16] This is not surprising as the relationship between consumer perceptions, behaviors, and their financial impact is very complex and requires a lot of data and understanding of the dynamics of the brand value chain. Analysts are much more comfortable in analyzing the financial results of brand and marketing impacts than linking market research data directly to financial results. In addition, the communication with investors focuses on financial ratios such as EPS, P/E, revenue and profit growth, operating and free cash flow, and ROE. Interestingly, the companies that own the brands have become increasingly sophisticated in tracking and analyzing the value creation of their brands and the return that their marketing investments and initiatives generate. Senior management of most companies now require detailed reporting on the performance and value creation of the company's brand assets. Most CEOs have embraced the notion of brands being key business assets that require specific management attention. Many companies have included brand value as a key performance indicator into their reporting and remuneration process. At the same time they have limited interest in reporting details on their intangible assets that can communicate sensitive information to competitors.

So should investors care about the value of brands and other intangibles? According to the research mentioned above probably yes. The announcement of brand values in the published rankings may not have a direct impact in moving share prices but stocks of companies with strong brands and high brand value outperform the rest of the market. This means investors implicitly recognize and value the contributions brands make to the underlying business. This should be sufficient evidence for investors to care about the value creation of brands which for many companies are the single most important asset. Given the impact and importance of brand assets they should be treated with similar if not more interest and attention than a companies' tangible asset base. A deeper and clearer understanding of the value creation of brands would benefit investors in selecting their stocks. After all investors rely on the credibility of brands to assure them that the underlying business can deliver the cash flows in the future.

CHAPTER 15

MANAGING BRAND VALUE

The importance of brands as corporate assets is now embraced by most leading companies around the world. Many CEOs are convinced that their brand or brands are key to the success of their business. The publicly available brand rankings most notably the "Best Global Brands" survey published annually in *BusinessWeek* have put the brand on the c-suite agenda. As marketing research techniques have advanced and sophisticated statistical models are able to process a large amount of data, companies have much better information about their brands than ever before. However, with increasing sophistication and insights on the value creation of brands within companies comes the realization that brands are rather complex assets that can defy traditional management structures.

In the old days there were broadly two brand management models. There were the traditional brand conglomerates such as Procter & Gamble, Unilever, Nestlé, The Coca-Cola Company, PepsiCo, Henkel Beiersdorf, and L'Oréal, that owned a large portfolio of consumer brands that were managed by dedicated brand managers. The focus of brand management was to use, in the main, communications such as advertising, sales promotions, and depending on the product a certain level of R&D and innovation to increase sales and contribution of each brand within a given budget. The brands were mainly or exclusively sold through retail intermediaries – direct customer contact was limited to classic media communication, packaging, and some point of sale activity. The key value drivers were communications, price, and some type of product innovation. The brands were managed on brand category and country level. The average tenure of a brand manager was about 2 years. The core brand positioning and values were set but had to be adjusted to changing consumer preferences and competitors' activities. P&G, Nestlé, and others established comprehensive brand management guidelines which became the text books for brand management worldwide. The key value drivers of the brand conglomerates were individual product brands with a very narrow focus to maintain differentiation and relevance within their respective categories. In some cases product brand and corporate brand were separate (P&G, Unilever) in others there was an overlap between a major product brand and the corporate brand such as Coca-Cola, PepsiCo, Kellogg's, Gillette, and Kraft. While in some cases one brand dominated the company's revenues and profits the focus was on the management of a large portfolio of brands. Even the Coca-Cola Company owns more than 400 brands. The size of many of these brand portfolios became hard to manage. Many of these brand conglomerates have started to focus on their top earning brands and established global management structures around them. They also have applied a value focus to their portfolio and culled underperforming brands. In 2000, Unilever initiated a restructuring program named "Path to Growth" that was to decrease the company's structural complexity, reduce costs, and increase efficiency by concentrating on 400 core brands that accounted for about 75 percent of company revenues. By 2004, Unilever had reduced its portfolio from 1,600 brands to 400 core brands. Today, Unilever has 12 brands, up from four brands in 1999, which generate sales over €1 billion. These include Knorr, Dove, Hellman's, Lipton, and Bird's Eye.[1] In 2008 the company achieved an operating margin of 17.6 percent compared with 11.2 percent in 1999. The Unilever case shows how the complexity of over-sized brand portfolios can be detrimental to profit margins and that a shift towards a more focused portfolio of global brands can deliver substantial improvements in the financial performance.

Next to the consumer brand conglomerates that manage large brand portfolios are the companies that focus on the management of one core master brand where product brand and corporate brand overlap such as IBM, Samsung, Nokia, GE, McDonald's, Nike, Accenture, Apple, and HSBC. There are also hybrids that own a small portfolio but are clearly dominated by one brand such as BMW and Disney. Here brand management has become more complex as it embraces all of the company's activities and involves all stakeholders including customers, employees, investors, suppliers, and regulators. Until the 1980s these companies focused their branding efforts on customers and consumers. With the emergence of corporate identity and internal branding brand management has become more comprehensive and sophisticated. Many companies realized that the brand is a valuable asset that affects many areas of the business particularly customer-focused activities. Due to the complexity of the brand impact within the business, master brand-focused companies have developed a different level of depth and integration of branding in the overall business process. However, due to management and budget silos the management of the brand is, in most companies, still fragmented. The key brand management tasks are still focused on media communications, web presence, sponsorship, and corporate identity and are housed in the marketing function. An important part of branding is the customer experience with the brand. Functions that are closely involved with the experience are sales, customer service, and R&D and product development. In many companies these are managed separately. They are informed by the marketing department and consult with them but are rarely integrated. Branding also impacts employee communications and engagement as the company's core values need to be understood, represented, and delivered by their employees. This is particularly important for service businesses where most employees are customer-facing and represent a key part of the customer experience. There is also the blurring of brand and reputation in particular at the corporate brand level. This touches on the investor relation function which deals with communication with the company's capital providers. While a change in corporate identity and positioning often involves senior management and, in many companies the CEO is claimed the brand custodian, the on-going management of the brand tends to fall to the marketing department with a focus on media communications. This is also due to the fact that the communications budget is the largest brand-only investment in most businesses. While other investments such as product development, R&D, sales force and customer service training, and retail investments do influence brand delivery they are at the same time focused on the overall operation of the business. The difficulty of clearly identifying the brand-related activities makes it hard to compartmentalize the brand management in one function.

A brand in its entirety impacts on all the customer-facing activities that create the customer experience of the brand. Therefore, it needs to be managed by someone in a senior position in the company. Ideally, the brand should be championed, sponsored and supported by the CEO of the company. This provides the gravitas needed to find support for the brand within the whole organization. The starting point should be a clear assessment of the value the brand creates for the underlying business. This needs to be done in an itemized manner in order to identify the brand's value contribution to the different customer segments.

The result of a detailed brand valuation will be an understanding of the overall value contribution of the brand to shareholder value as well as the breakdown of its value by strategic customer segments. The segmentation should be based on customer relevant profit effective factors. These may include attitudes, behaviors, product or service, and geography. The value drivers of the brand need to be linked to the different operations of the business such as marketing, sales, customer service, and product development/R&D. Once the impact and relevance of the brand for each function has been identified the responsibility in building the brand needs to be determined for each operational function. The brand is most effectively managed by a senior manager at board level or with a direct reporting line to the CEO and the Board such as a Chief Marketing Officer (CMO) or the Head of corporate strategy. This integrates the brand directly with the customer-facing and impacting operational functions and avoids it being pushed down into the communication functions. It also allows for integrated brand planning and delivery throughout the customer experience. Ultimately, brand management needs to control the customer experience from strategy development to customer touch point execution. It is therefore useful to have all customer-facing activities under one senior report. Many companies such as Samsung have created a strong CMO role that has been very successful in integrating all brand and customer-facing functions into a globally-managed team.[2]

The value creation of the brand needs to be communicated and explained to employees and senior management in order to make them understand the importance of the brand for their company. Brand value is also a great crystallization point for the success and performance of the brand. The financial value makes a clear statement about the success of the company's brand-building efforts. It can also act as a strong "rallying call" that can unite all employees. It is much easier to understand and measure the impact of the value of the brand compared to a complex set of metrics such as awareness, consideration, and choice. These important metrics that constitute the brand value chain are crucial in measuring brand performance. However, they are not as powerful and clear as the overall economic value of the brand. Next to communications the value of the brand needs to be integrated into the company's performance metrics as a key performance indicator (KPI) along with other core metrics that drive the brand value chain. These metrics depend on the nature of the business and its specific brand value drivers. For example, a packaged goods brand will focus its metrics on consumer attitudes and behaviors while a service brand will also look at customer service delivery, customer turnover, and advocacy. The metrics set are adopted according to the impact and relevance the specific function or department has on brand value. For example, product development and R&D directly influence product-driven perceptions such as quality, reliability, and design but not point of sale promotions or customer service. Their brand KPIs should therefore focus on their specific inputs. The communications function is responsible for all media communications as well as corporate identity. Its KPIs would therefore include effectiveness metrics for advertising, web presence, and other communications. Brand value should also become a cornerstone of the company's ROI assessment and capital allocation process. Given the sophistication and process that is applied to the investments in physical assets such as land, plant, or machinery, or investments in IT and process engineering it makes sense to apply the same efforts to investments in the brand which constitute one of the most valuable assets of the business. Return on brand investments, as described in Chapter 13, does not only refer to media communications but to all activities that build and deliver the brand experience physically as well as psychologically. In many cases non-media expenses such as product design, retail environment, customer service, or sales force training and education can be more important in brand-building than some advertising campaigns or sales promotions. Brand-building needs to be approached and managed with the same rigor and diligence as other asset investments such as capital expenditures. Planning, measuring, and executing brand investments need to follow similar procedures. This also requires an understanding and endorsement of the role and value of the brand asset within the company by its senior management. Brand value has a key role as it provides a value that is comparable to other business assets. The brand can therefore be integrated into an overall value-based management approach that puts the brand on an equal footing with other business assets. It must be remembered that the value generation of capital investments is not a stand-alone affair but works in the context of the other business assets such as brand, people, and processes. The same is true for the brand as it creates value in the context of other business assets. Brand value enables the company to manage the brand asset according to its long-term and sustainable value creation. Samsung Electronics exemplifies how the notion of understanding and managing the brand as a key corporate asset can build sustainable brand and business value.

After a careful analysis of the companies' market position its chairman realized that in order to move up the value chain beyond its original equipment manufacturer (OEM) status the company needed to build its own brand and R&D capabilities. Samsung Chairman Lee Kun-Hee wanted to implement "strategies that can raise brand value, which is a leading intangible asset and the source of corporate competitiveness, to the global level."[3] The company embarked on a detailed analysis on the value of its brand, its competitive position, and value drivers. Based on this analysis the chairman announced brand value as key corporate performance indicator (KPI) and set brand value targets. These targets then formed part of the management review and remuneration assessment.[4] The value focus enabled Samsung to obtain "buy-in" for its brand investments, such as its Olympic sponsorship as well as its other marketing initiatives, from senior management, employees, and shareholders. The rise and value creation of the Samsung brand is one of the largest corporate success stories of the twenty-first century. Within a period of 5 years the brand had overtaken Panasonic and Sony to become the global number two in mobile phones and the leader in memory chips and plasma screens. Samsung is therefore a formidable example in the use of a disciplined and value-based brand-management approach that can transform a business and create substantial shareholder value.

Another aspect of brand management is employees' performance and remuneration assessment. To make the brand asset relevant to employees they need not only to know about the value of the brand to the business but they also need to become responsible and accountable for building and maintaining the brand. Brand value, specific job responsibilities, and specific brand impacting elements need to be included in the employee review process. This should be done by integrating and linking employee actions to brand asset building efforts rather than scoring them against a list of brand value criteria. For example, a specific product design has sold well but research also indicates that it has affected consumer's perception about the brand. Apple's and Samsung's product designs are not only slick and aesthetically pleasing they also differentiate and build the perceptions of the respective brands. Product designers are given brand positioning and values as a framework and guidelines for their product design but it is their creativity and effort that converts the brand into a tangible product. This brand-building momentum needs to be captured and rewarded. The brand-building

efforts of employees should be integrated into annual reviews, promotions, and remuneration. At Samsung senior marketing officers received
their bonuses partly according to meeting brand value targets set by the
company's chairman. Most B2B and service brands depend heavily on
the behaviors of employees. It therefore makes sense to link their performance assessment and remuneration to their brand asset-building
activities.

For brand conglomerates that manage a large portfolio of consumer
brands the focus of brand management remains on the product level
as product and organizational brands perform very different tasks. In
some case very large brands such as Gillette and Nivea are managed
with a significant level of independence and run almost as independent
businesses that command significant brand loyalty from their employees. In the management of brand conglomerates it is fundamentally
important to keep the management of different brands separate even
when manufacturing, R&D, distribution, and media buying are shared.
The case of the Gucci and YSL brands is a good example. As long as
Tom Ford was managing both brands simultaneously the positioning
of YSL remained too close to Gucci to develop its own sufficiently
distinct image. Despite its significantly higher price points the brand
has, so far, failed to provide positive returns to the Gucci Group. On
the other hand large portfolios can lead to management complexities
that become easily detrimental to shareholder value creation as mentioned previously. It is therefore important to ensure that the most
valuable brands are not impaired by too much management focus and
resource allocation on the large amount of small brands. A brand value
focus helps to ensure that the most valuable brands in the portfolio
are developed and invested in while brands that are value-draining
and absorb disproportionate management time and resources are
weeded out.

The following management tasks will enable the optimal economic
value creation of brand assets:

- The CEO and senior management understand and manage the
  brand(s) as a key business asset. They see the brand as a holistic asset
  that needs to involve and engage all of the company's activities most
  notably those that are customer-facing.
- The business functions and teams that manage the brand strategically and on a day-to-day basis understand the impact of the

brand on the company's business and customers' purchase decisions. Their remuneration and promotion is linked to brand value creation.

- The brand is managed in an integrated fashion involving all brand delivery relevant functions and tasks and not left to the marketing department dealing with communications.
- The brand meets and stays relevant to customer need and provides them with benefits in a distinctive and differentiated manner expressed in the brand's positioning.
- The brand is consistently communicated and delivered through all customer-facing touch points.
- The pricing strategy is aligned with customers' perception of value. The price is regarded as fair and appropriate for the benefits the brand provides.
- The brand is developed, built, and invested in according to its long-term value creation within the business. Brand investments are consistent and accumulative drawing in all customer touch points. Brand investments are made according to their long-term value creation.
- The brand's value creation is monitored and managed according to the brand value chain and all its key components culminate in the brand's economic value.
- In the case of the multiple brands or a brand portfolio the relationship of the brands is set and managed according to their economic value generation.

Brand value focused management is a formidable way to create sustainable shareholder value as evidenced by Samsung and many other leading companies around the world. As the value of the brand is the quantification of the brand's value creation from consumer perception to financial value it captures all value-creating brand elements. Brand value puts the brand on an equal footing with other company assets and enables the company to understand the value creation of the brand in the context of and relative to other business assets. This allows optimization of capital allocation according to the interplay and relative contribution of all assets. The brand is an asset that needs to be invested in and managed in a similar fashion to other capital investments. Brand value recognizes that the majority of brand value is generated in the future. Brand value is thus the most appropriate approach to assess return on brand investments and communicate the importance of the brand to internal and external audiences. Companies can use brand value to rally employees and instill a brand-focused set of behaviors and overall culture particularly in the customer-facing departments.

CONCLUSION

The various aspects of brand value creation demonstrate that both the business and finance communities acknowledge the economic value of branding. The brand generates and secures a loyal customer base with the related cash flow. The brand enables companies to enter new markets and shift their business focus to adapt to changing market conditions. The brand is one of the few business assets that if properly managed and invested in, can appreciate in value on an on-going basis. The brand is one of the most sustainable assets and can outlive the average corporation. Of the leading global 100 brands about 70 percent have existed for longer than 50 years with most of the younger brands emerging in new categories such as IT and the Internet. It also shows that brands can maintain a leadership position over a sustained period as evidenced by brands such as Coca-Cola, IBM, Gillette, Louis Vuitton, and Goldman Sachs. Brands help companies to outperform rivals on the stock market. Companies with strong brands generate higher returns at a lower risk compared to competitors and market indices.

In many companies brands now account for the majority of shareholder value as evidenced by the development of price to book ratios and the values published by various consulting firms. The brand rankings published annually in *BusinessWeek* have raised the awareness, in the board room, of the importance of brands for shareholder value creation. The balance sheet recognition of brands and other intangible assets may be an unsatisfactory solution for dealing with brand value but it is a first step in trying to include brands in a company's reporting framework. Many CEOs now understand and emphasize the crucial role that a brand has in their business.

The example of Samsung has demonstrated how a brand-value based management approach can create a leading global brand in the top quartile in less than a decade. The company used brand value as the starting point and as a key success metric throughout its global brand building process. The value of the Samsung brand was at the core of its marketing activities. The company's chairman set brand value targets. Marketing investments exceeding US$1 billion per year were guided and allocated to maximize brand value creation. The value of the Samsung brand was established as core KPI most notably for senior marketing executives. Since 2000, the value of the Samsung brand as published in the *BusinessWeek* annual brand ranking has grown from US$5.2 billion to US$17.5 in 2009. In the same period Samsung Electronics' share price has grown in excess of 250 percent while at the same time Sony's share price declined by nearly 175 percent. While there were many other factors at play the brand value focus was a key element in Samsung's success story.

Brand value has become a key value driver for exploiting and building a company's intangible asset base. Increasingly companies use brands to earn income from licensing brands to third parties in markets they do not wish to invest in directly. Many multinational corporations consolidate their brand and strategic marketing activities in dedicated special purpose brand management companies to manage and transfer the intellectual property to the operating companies more effectively. This converts the marketing function from a cost to a profit centre. It increases the efficiency of brand management through centralization and enables companies to optimize their global tax position. Brands are also increasingly used in the largest IP securitizations. Due to their proven cash flow generating ability, brand assets have raised debt facilities exceeding US$1 billion. The brand(s) guarantees and secures the servicing and repayment of the debt thus reducing the financing costs due to the lower risk profile of their cash flows. This is an application that will significantly increase in the future as investors become more comfortable and fluent with brand-secured debt facilities.

With companies being aware of the value of their brand assets and marketing investments, amounting in many cases to more than half of the cost of goods sold (COGS), there has been an increasing need to identify and quantify the return on investments made into brands most notably the traditional marketing and communications expenses. The easy availability of short-term sales data from scanners has led many companies to shift their marketing budget towards short-term sales effective marketing activities such as direct mail, the Internet, and sales promotions. While these investments benefit from short-term accountability they ignore the accumulative long-term effect of brand image-building investments. In addition, in many businesses significant brand value is also created by activities that do not fall into the responsibility of the marketing department such as R&D, customer service, and sales force training and management. A brand-value based return on investment approach as described in Chapter 9 provides an ROI assessment of all brand relevant investments according to their short-term and long-term value creation. Many leading companies have successfully implemented such a brand-focused ROI approach that captures the holistic nature of many brand investments. Most companies have sufficient marketing and financial data available to implement a brand ROI approach. If not, a reallocation of the research budget would enable the creation of the necessary data without additional costs.

Brand value has also been the focus of many prominent M&A and LBO transactions. It was the takeover bid of RHM in the UK that triggered the recognition of the brand as economic asset and its reporting on the balance sheet. In many transactions the brand has become a key asset to be recognized in the value assessment. In corporate mergers, brand value helps to determine the optimal branding strategy for the combined operations. When the acquisition is completed, the value of the acquired brand assets needs to be capitalized on the balance sheet and subjected to an annual impairment test.

The issue about disclosure of the value of brands and other intangibles is not solved by the current accounting standards which focus on acquired goodwill only. While the debate has focused on the discrepancy between the value of acquired brands that are recognized on the balance sheet and that of internally generated brands that are not reported, the real issue is whether the balance sheet is the appropriate place to deal with the issue. In order to properly account for the fair value of each asset, companies would have to prepare cash flow valuations for each asset that would produce a total close to the market value of the company. Companies will be reluctant to do so because this implies providing earnings guidance far into the future, which will require management to explain to investors the value difference between the management's and the stock market's valuation of the business. While the gap will probably be significantly lower than the current price to book ratio it would result in management claiming to have a different view on the company's future than the market. Although an interesting concept, it is highly unlikely that management boards would be willing to undergo such a level of scrutiny and accountability. Nevertheless, more disclosure of companies' brand assets would provide useful investor information in particular if the brand(s) accounts for the majority of shareholder value. A statement on the value of the brand(s) is an opportunity to close the value reporting gap. Companies are already happy to quote brand values published in *BusinessWeek's* annual brand ranking. Looking to the future there will be more requirements for companies to disclose the value of their brands and other intangible assets. However, how long this will take is difficult to foresee. The accounting debate on intangible assets continued for about a decade until adjustments were implemented.

The understanding and recognition of the economic value of brands is a relative recent phenomenon. It was the increasing goodwill in M&A transactions in the late 1980s which were at odds with the accounting regimes at the time. This led to the development of brand valuation methodologies and the recognition of acquired brands and other intangible assets on the balance sheet according to all leading accounting standards. At the same time the term brand equity emerged from the marketing community to capture the concept of the long-term impact of brands on customers and revenue generation. The integration of the contributions from the marketing and financial communities into a brand value method and framework as outlined in this book has led to the recognition of brands as a key economic asset. This approach is based on established and proven concepts and models from the marketing and financial communities. It complies with accepted principles of corporate finance and provides a value comparable to other business assets as well as the overall value of the business. Despite the integration of all the sophisticated and advanced marketing and financial analyses, assessing the economic value of brands requires judgement and experience, although this is true for most forward-looking valuations. With up to 80 percent of a company's stock market value depending on cash flows expected beyond the third year of forecast investors rely heavily on assumptions about the future which can change very quickly and dramatically as evidenced by the stock market developments between 2007 and 2009. Despite the sophistication of advanced and complex trading programs that analyze large amounts of data in seconds or less, most experts got their assumptions wrong and lost unprecedented amounts on their share investments. This lies in the nature of valuation which is most appropriately expressed by Warren Buffet, one of the world's most successful investors, when he said "price is what you pay and value is what you get." In this context the valuation of brands has held up rather impressively. Valuing brands is not unlike valuing other assets – an expert assessment based on best available data processed through a transparent and proven analytical framework to derive the future cash flows the asset is expected to generate.

So with brands accounting for a substantial portion of shareholder value and brand metrics and valuation tools available to measure and manage this value companies have started to embrace a value-based approach to managing their brand assets. This means that brand building and management is not confined to the marketing department but is an activity of the whole company and in particular its consumer-focused or customer-facing operations. In many companies the senior management, including the CEO, have become brand aware and focused. That does not mean the end of all corporate silos and budget fights but a much better base for making brand decisions than in the past. For analysts and investors, brand value provides some interesting and relevant insights about the share price performance and potential of the brand-owning firms. This should lead to more interest in the value of brands in the future.

NOTES

Chapter 1   What is a brand?

1. Tom Blackett, 2003, p. 14.
2. Karl Moore and Susan Reid, 2008, pp. 24–5.
3. Stefan Schwarzkopf, 2008, p. 13.
4. American Marketing Association, AMA 2006.
5. Philip Kottler, 2001 p. 188.
6. Stephen Northcutt, 2007.
7. David Aaker, 1991.
8. Charles Forelle, 2009.
9. The World Customs Organization, Organisation for Economic Co-operation and Development.
10. Frederick Balfour, 2005.

Chapter 2   The value of brands

1. John A. Quelch and Katherine E. Jocz, 2009.
2. Sundar S. Bharadwaj, 2008.
3. Peter F. Drucker, 1954, p. 32.
4. Michael E. Porter, 1985.
5. Associated Press, 2008.
6. International Bottled Water Association and the Beverage Marketing Corporation, 2008.
7. *Which* online.
8. *Women's Wear Daily*, 2008.
9. Philip Kottler and Waldemar Pförtsch, 2006.
10. *Investment Dealer's Digest*, 2003.
11. Eric S. Raymond, 2003.
12. Burson-Marstellar, 2008.
13. Frank Fehle, Susan M. Fournier, Thomas J. Madden and David G.T. Shrider, 2008; T. Madden, F. Fehle and S. Fournier, 2006.
14. Tara Kalwarski, 2009.
15. *Financial Times*, 2009; Mark Ritson, 2009.
16. Pernod Ricard, 2008.
17. AT&T Inc., 2005.

Chapter 3 Assessing the value of brands

1. Tony McAuley, 2003.
2. David Aaker, 1991b.
3. Kevin Lane Keller, 1997.

Chapter 4 Brand equity: the marketer's view on brand value

1. David Aaker, 1996a.
2. David Aaker, 1996a, p. 336.
3. Kevin Lane Keller, 2009.
4. see brandassetconsulting.com
5. BAV Electronics 2006.
6. Jonathan Knowles, 2003.
7. John Gerzeman and Ed Lebar, 2008; thebrandbubble.com
8. Deboo, 2007.
9. See brandz.com
10. See brandz.com
11. See brandz.com
12. See brandz.com; *Financial Times*, 2009.
13. FT Global Brands, 2009, p. 2.
14. David Muir, 2009, p. 2.
15. See *Financial Times*, 2009.
16. See Millward Brown, 2008.
17. See The Neilsen Company.
18. See http://www.ipsos-asi.com/pdf/rc5.pdf
19. Dave Walker, 2002.
20. See PricewaterhouseCoopers, 2008.
21. See Frederick F. Reichheld, 2003; bain.com

Chapter 5 Financial approaches to valuing brands

1. Bloomberg, 2007.
2. See Chapter 2.
3. See Chapter 2.
4. See Reuters.com; Best Global Brands, 2008; author's calculations.
5. See royaltysource.com
6. IVSC Discussion, 2007.

Chapter 6 Integrating finance and marketing: economic use method

1. Noel Penrose, 1989, pp. 37–9.
2. See Best Global Brands, 2009; Raymond Perrier (ed.), 1997, pp. 55–60; Brand Valuation, 2008.
3. Raymond Perrier (ed.), 1997, pp. 33, 43–53.
4. Best Canadian Brands, 2008.
5. see Best Global Brands, 2009.
6. "Global 500," 2009.

7. Anita Zednik and Andreas Strebinger, 2008; Best Global Brands 2009; Gabriella Salinas 2009.
8. See Markenbewertung – Die Tank AG, Absatzwirtschaft, 2004.
9. Tom Koller, Marc Goedhart and David Wessels, 2005, pp 277–8.
10. See *Financial Times*, 2009.
11. DIN ISO .
12. Brand Valuation Forum 2008.

Chapter 7   Brand valuation best practice approach

1. See Jacob Jacoby, 2001; Max H. Bazerman, 2001; Khalid Dubas, M. Dubas and Petur Jonsson, 2005.
2. Simon Bowers, 2009.

Chapter 8   Brands on the balance sheet

1. Lord Hanson, 2004; Hope Lambert, 1987; "Lord of the Raiders," 2004.
2. Lloyd Austin, 2007, pp. 64–5.
3. KPMG, 2007.
4. KPMG, 2007; PwC, 2008.
5. *IAS 38*.
6. Philip Little, David Coffee and Roger Lirely, 2005.

Chapter 9   Brand securitization

1. Nigel Jones and Ann Hoe, 2008.
2. John S. Hillery, 2004, p. 17.
3. Jan Eisbruck, 2008, p. 21.
4. Tonu McAuley, 2003.
5. *Euromoney* Magazine, 2006; Ambac Assurance Corporation, 2007.
6. Robert Berner, 2007, pp. 58–60.
7. nexcen.com

Chapter 10   Brand value in mergers & acquisitions

1. Gail Edmondson and David Welch, 2004.
2. Tom Buerkle, 1998.
3. Simon Bowers, 2009.
4. "Mother and Child Reunion: Will the AT&T/SBC Merger Build or Destroy Value?" 2005; Dr. Michael A. Noll, 2005.
5. AT&T Inc. 2005.
6. Liz Vaughan-Adams, 2001.

Chapter 11   Brand licensing

1. *Indiaprwire*, 2008.
2. Global Transfer Pricing Survey Ernst & Young 2009.
3. OECD.org

4. Top 100 Global Licensors, p. 38.
5. Jamie Huckbody, 2003.
6. See Reuters.com.

Chapter 12   The brand value chain

1. Kevin L. Keller and Donald R. Lehmann, 2003, p. 23.
2. McKinsey, 2003.
3. "Beyond Petroleum pays off for BP," 2008.
4. Paul K. Driesen, 2009.
5. John Quelch, and Anna Harrington, 2005.
6. Corporate Executive Board, 2009.
7. Times online 28 Jan 2008.
8. See Corporate Executive Board, 2009.

Chapter 13   Return on brand investment

1. See *Marketing Week* 3, October 2008, this quote has also been attributed to John Wannamaker and Henry Ford.
2. Prasad A. Naik, Kalyan Raman and Russell S. Winer, 2005, pp. 25–34.
3. Booz Allen Hamilton, 2006.
4. superbrands.net
5. E.F. Loftus and G.R Loftus, 1980; Kevin L. Keller, 1993, pp. 1–22.
6. Best Global Brands, 2008; *Financial Times*, 2009, PriceWaterhouseCoopers, Markenwert wird zunehmend als Unternehmenswert anerkannt, 2006; *Brand Leverage*, 1999; Peter Doyle, 2000.
7. Vithala R. Rao, Manoj K. Agarwal, and Denise Dahlhoff, 2004, pp. 126–41; Amit M. Joshi and Dominique M. Hanssens, 2007.
8. PriceWaterhouseCoopers, 2008a.
9. M.G. Dekimpe, and D. Hanssens, 1995, pp. 1–21.
10. Gert Assmus, Johan U. Farley, and Donald R. Lehmann, 1984, pp. 65–74; Chiquan Guo, 2003; Demetrios Vakratsa and Tim Ambler, 1999, pp. 26–43.
11. Robert E. Smith, 1993, pp. 204–19.
12. Joseph W. Alba and J. Wesley Hutchinson, 1987, pp. 411–54; Joseph W. Alba, J. Wesley Hutchinson and John G. Lynch, 1991, pp. 1–49.
13. R. J. Kent and C. T. Allen, 1994, pp. 97–105; Demetrios Vakratsas and Tim Ambler, 1999, pp. 26–43.
14. C. J. Cobb-Walgren, C. A. Ruble and N. Donthu, 1995, pp. 25–4.
15. Carl F. Mela, Sunil Gupta and Donald R. Lehmann, 1997, pp. 248–61.
16. Margaret C. Campbell and Kevin L. Keller, 2003, pp. 292–304; R. J. Kent and C. T. Allen, 1994, pp. 97–105.
17. Fang Wang, Xiao-Ping Zhang and Ming Ouyang, 2007.
18. *Financial Times*, 2 August 2003.
19. *Sports Business Daily*, 2006.
20. Kevin L. Keller, 1993, pp. 1–22.
21. G. Belch and A. Belch, 2004.
22. Singfat Chu Chu and Hean Tat Keh, 2006.

23. R. Berner and D. Kiley, 2005.
24. D.S. Tull, Van R. Wood, D. Duhan, T. Gillpatrick, K.R. Robertson, and J.G. Helgeson, 1986, pp. 25–32.
25. U. Ben-Zion, 1978, pp. 224–9; M. Corstjens, and J. Merrihue, 2003, pp. 114–21; Fang Wang, Xiao-Ping Zhang and Ming Ouyang, 2007.
26. Y.K. Ho, H.T. Keh and J. Ong, 2005, pp. 3–14.
27. A. Chaudhuri, 2002, pp. 33–43.
28. Singfat Chu Chu and Hean Tat Keh, 2006.
29. Berk Ataman, Harald J. van Heerde and Carl F. Mela, 2006.
30. "An Analytic Approach to Balancing Marketing and Branding ROI," 2007.
31. Tom Koller, Marc Goedhart, David Wessels, 2005, pp. 277–8; Mckinsey 2004.
32. John Quelch and Anna Harrington 2005; Best Global Brands, 2002; M. Corstjens and J. Merrihue, 2003, pp. 114–21; R. Berner and D. Kiley, 2005, pp. 56–63; Kris Frieswick, 2001.

Chapter 14   Brands and the stock market

1. Tom Koller, Marc Goedhart, David Wessels, 2005, pp. 277–8; Frank Fehle, Susan M. Fournier, Thomas J. Madden and David G.T. Shrider, 2008; T. Madden, F. Fehle and S. Fournier, 2006; Mckinsey, 2004.
2. Best Global Brands, 2009, PricewaterhouseCoopers, 2006; "Brand Leverage," 1999; Peter Doyle, 2000.
3. The Coca-Cola Company, 2008.
4. Martin Deboo, 2007, pp. 28–31; Morgan Stanley, 1995.
5. David A. Aaker and Robert Jacobson, 1994; "Study Shows Brand-building Pays off for Stockholders," 1994, p.18.
6. Frank Fehle, Susan M. Fournier, Thomas J. Madden and David G.T. Shrider, 2008; T. Madden, F. Fehle and S. Fournier, 2006.
7. BrandZ, 2009.
8. Natalya Delcoure, 2008; D. Horsky, and P. Swyngedouw, 1987, pp. 320–35.
9. P. Chaney, T. Devinney and R. Winer, 1991, pp. 573–610.
10. David A. Aaker, and R. Jacobson, 2001.
11. David A. Aaker, and R. Jacobson, 1994; S. Moorthy and H. Zhao, 2000, pp. 221–33.
12. I.E. Berger, and A.A. Mitchell, 1989, pp. 269–79.
13. C.J. Cobb-Walgren, C.A. Ruble, and N. Donthu, 1995.
14. Shuba Srinivasan and Dominique M. Hanssens, 2009.
15. Best Global Brands, 2008.
16. "How Analysts View Marketing," 2005.

Chapter 15   Managing brand value

1. Nikhil Bahadur, Edward Landry and Steven Treppo, 2006.
2. John Quelch and Anna Harrington, 2005.
3. Samsung, 2007.
4. Samsung 2007.

BIBLIOGRAPHY

D. Aaker, *Building Strong Brands* (New York: Free Press, 1991a).

D. Aaker, *Managing Brand Equity* (New York: Free Press, 1991b).

D. Aaker, *Building Strong Brands* (New York: Free Press, 1996), p. 336.

D. A. Aaker and R. Jacobson, "The Financial Information Content of Perceived Quality," *Journal of Marketing Research*, 31, 1994.

D. A. Aaker and R. Jacobson, "The Value Relevance of Brand Attitude in High Technology Markets," *Journal of Marketing Research*, 38 (November), 2001, 485–93.

J. W. Alba and J. W. Hutchinson, "Dimensions of Consumer Expertise," *Journal of Consumer Research*, 13, 1987, 411–54.

J. W. Alba, J. W. Hutchinson and J. G. Lynch, Memory and Decision Making, in: H. H. Kassarjian and T. S. Robertson (eds) *Perspectives in Consumer Behavior*, 4th edn (New York: Prentice-Hall, 1991), pp. 1–49.

Ambac Assurance Corporation, "Dunkin' Brands Securitization Marks Milestone for Innovative Private Equity Financing 2007," New York, 2007.

American Marketing Association (AMA) 2006, retrieved from: marketingpower. com.

"An Analytic Approach to Balancing Marketing and Branding ROI," 2007, retrieved from: Enumerys.com.

B. Ataman, H. J. van Heerde and C. F. Mela, "The Long-term Effect of Marketing Strategy on Brand Performance," 2006, available at: http://www.zibs.com/techreports/The%20Long-term%20Effect%20of%20Marketing%20Strategy.pdf.

AT&T Inc. Annual Report, 2005.

G. Assmus, J. U. Farley, and D. R. Lehmann, "How Advertising Affects Sales: Meta-Analysis of Econometric Results," *Journal of Marketing Research*, 21 (February), 1984, 65–74.

Associated Press, "Honda, Porsche Lead in J. D. Power Quality Study," June 4, 2008.

L. Austin, "Accounting for Intangible Assets," *University of Auckland Business Review*, 9 (1), 2007, 64–5.

N. Bahadur, E. Landry, and S. Treppo, "How to Slim Down a Brand Portfolio," McLean, VA: Booz Allen, 15 November 2006.

F. Balfour, Fakes! "The Global Counterfeit Business is Out of Control, Targeting Everything from Computer Chips to Life-saving Machines," *BusinessWeek*, February 7, 2005, available at: http://www.businessweek.com/magazine/content/05_06/b3919001_mz001.htm

BAV Electronics 2006 results, available at: brandassetvaluator.com.au.

M. H. Bazerman, "Is There Help for the Big Ticket Buyer?" Boston, MA: Harvard College, September 17, 2001.

G. Belch and A. Belch, *Advertising and Promotion: An Integrated Marketing Communications Perspective* (New York: McGraw Hill, 2004).

U. Ben-Zion, "The Investment Aspect of Non-production Expenditures: An Empirical Test," *Journal of Economics and Business*, 30 (3), 1978, 224–9.

I. E. Berger and A. A. Mitchell, "The Effect of Advertising on Attitude Accessibility, Attitude Confidence, and the Attitude-behavior Relationship," *Journal of Consumer Research*, 16 (December) 1989, 269–79.

R. Berner, "The New Alchemy at Sears," *BusinessWeek*, April 16, 2007, 58–60.

R. Berner and D. Kiley, "Global Brands," *BusinessWeek*, 5 (12), 2005, 56–63.

Best Global Brand, 2002, *BusinessWeek*, August 5, 2002.

Best Global Brand, 2008, *BusinessWeek*, September 29, 2008.

Best Global Brands, 2009, *Financial Times*, April 29, 2009.

Best Canadian Brands, 2008, available at: Interbrand.com.

"Beyond Petroleum Pays Off For BP," *Environmental Leader*, January 15, 2008.

S. Bharadwai, "The Mystery and Motivation of Valuing Brands in M&A," November 13, 2008, Atlanta, GA: knowledge@emory.

T. Blackett, *What is a Brand? Brands and Branding* (London: Profile Books, 2003), p. 14.

Bloomberg, February 26, 2007, available at: www.bloomberg.com.

Booz & Co., "The Future of Advertising: Implications for Marketing and Media," February, McLean, VA: Booz Allen, 2006.

S. Bowers, "Woolworth Lives Again as Online Brand," *The Guardian*, February 2, 2009.

"Brand Leverage," *McKinsey Quarterly*, May 1999, available at: Mckinsey.com.

"Brand Valuation: The Key to Unlock the Benefits from your Brand Asset," Interbrand, 2008.

Brand Valuation Forum, "10 Principles of Monetary Brand Valuation," Berlin, June 18, 2008.

BrandZ "Top 100 Most Valuable Global brands 2009," Millward Brown Optimor, available at: millwardbrown.com.

T. Buerkle, "BMW Wrests Rolls-Royce Name Away From VW," *The New York Times*, July 29, 1998.

Burson-Marstellar, "Most Prized Reputation Rankings," July 17, 2008, available at: http://www.burson-marsteller.com/Innovation_and_insights/blogs_and_podcasts/BM_Blog/Lists/Posts/Post.aspx?List=75c7a224-05a3-4f25-9ce5-2a90a7c0c761&ID=45.

M. C. Campbell and K. L. Keller, "Brand Familiarity and Advertising Repetition Effects," *Journal of Consumer Research*, 3 (September), 2003, 292–304.

P. Chaney, T. Devinney and R. Winer, "The Impact of New Product Introductions on the Market Value of Firms," *Journal of Business*, 64, 1991, 573–610.

A. Chaudhuri, "How Brand Reputation Affects the Advertising-brand Equity Link," *Journal of Advertising Research*, 42, 2002, 33–43.

S. C. Chu, and H. T. Keh, *Brand Value Creation: Analysis of the Interbrand-BusinessWeek Brand Value Rankings* (Berlin, Springer Science, 2006).

C. J. Cobb-Walgren, C. A. Ruble and N. Donthu, "Brand Equity, Brand Preference, and Purchase Intent," *Journal of Advertising*, 24 (3), 1995, 25–4.

Coca-Cola Company, The, Annual Report 2008, available at: http://www.thecoca-colacompany.com/investors/form_10K_2008.html.

Corporate Executive Board, "What companies do best, 2009" *BusinessWeek*, June 23, 2009.

M. Corstjens and J. Merrihue, "Optimal Marketing," *Harvard Business Review*, 81, (October) 2003, 114–21.

M. Deboo, "Ad Metrics and Stock Markets: How to Bridge the Yawning Gap," *Admap*, 484, June, 2007, 28–31.

M. G. Dekimpe and D. Hanssens, "The Persistence of Marketing Effects on Sales," *Marketing Science*, 14, 1995, 1–21.

N. Delcoure, *Corporate Branding and Shareholders' Wealth* (Huntsville, TX: Sam Houston State University, 2008).

DIN ISO Project Brand Valuation, available at: www.din.de.

"Do Fundamentals Really Drive the Stock Market?" 2004, available at: Mckinsey.com.

P. Doyle, *Value-Based Marketing* (New York: John Wiley & Sons, 2000).

P. K. Driesen, "BP-Back to Petroleum," *IPA Review*, March 2009.

P. F. Drucker, *The Practice of Management* (Harper & Brothers, New York, 1954) p. 32.

K. Dubas, M. Dubas and P. Jonsson, "Rationality in Consumer Decision Making," Proceedings of the Academy of Marketing Studies, 10, 2, Las Vegas, 2005.

G. Edmondson and D. Welch, "VW Steals a Lead in Luxury," *BusinessWeek*, December 6, 2004.

Eisbruck, Jan, "Introduction Royal(ty) Succession: The Evolution of IP-backed Securitisation, Building and Enforcing Intellectual Property Value 2008," 21, Moody's Investors Service.

Euromoney Magazine, July 18, 2006.

F. Fehle, S. M. Fournier, T. J. Madden and D. G. T. Shrider, "Brand Value and Asset Pricing," *Quarterly Journal of Finance and Accounting*, January 1, 2008.

Financial Times, Invasion, August 2, 2003.

Financial Times, "Global Brands," FT Special Report, April 29, 2009.

C. Forelle, "Europe's High Court Tries on a Bunny Suit Made of Chocolate," *WSJ*, June 11, 2009.

K. Frieswick, "New Brand Day:Attempts to Gauge the ROI of Advertising Hinge on Determining a Brand's Overall Value," November 1 2001, available at: CFO.com.

J. Gerzema, and E. Lebar, *Brand Bubble: The Looming Crisis in Brand Value and How to Avoid It* (New York: John Wiley & Sons, 2008).

"Global 500," *BrandFinance*, April 2009, available at: brandfinance.com.

C. Guo, "Co-integration Analysis of the Aggregate Advertising-consumption Relationship," *Journal of the Academy of Business and Economics*, February 2003.

J. S. Hillery, "Securitization of Intellectual Property: Recent Trends from the United States," Washington/Core, March 2004, p. 17.

Y. K. Ho, H. T. Keh and J. Ong, "The Effects of R&D and Advertising on Firm Value: An Examination of Manufacturing and Non-manufacturing Firms," *IEEE Transactions on Engineering Management*, 52, 2005, 3–14.

D. Horsky and P. Swyngedouw, "Does it Pay to Change Your Company's Name? A Stock Market Perspective," *Marketing Science*, 6 (4), 1987, 320–35.

"How Analysts View Marketing," IPA report, July 28, 2005.

J. Huckbody, "Pierre Cardin, He's Everywhere," *Fairfax Digital*, August 1, 2003

IAS 38, International Accounting Standards Board, available at: www.iasb.org.

Indiaprwire, "Brand Licensing to be the Next Big Thing in India," October 11, 2008.

Interbrand.com.

International Bottled Water Association and the Beverage Marketing Corporation, 2008, available at: www. botteledwater.org.

International Valuation Standards Council (IVSC) Discussion, "Determination of Fair Value of Intangible Assets for IFRS Reporting Purposes Paper," July 2007.

Investment Dealer's Digest, "The Scramble to Brand: Not all Wall Street Banks are Equal – or Are They?" October 27, 2003.

J. Jacoby, *Is it Rational to Assume Consumer Rationality? Some Consumer Psychological Perspectives on Rational Choice Theory* (New York: Leonard N. Stern Graduate School of Business, 2001).

"J. D. Power Quality Study," The Associated Press, June 4, 2008.

N. Jones and A. Hoe, "IP-backed Securitisation: Realising the Potential," *Linkelaters,* 2008.

A. M. Joshi and D. M. Hanssens, "Advertising Spending and Market Capitalization," working paper, UCLA Anderson School of Management, April 2007.

T. Kalwarski, "Investing in Brands," *BusinessWeek,* July 23, 2009.

K. L. Keller, "Conceptualizing, Measuring, and Managing Customer-based Brand Equity," Journal of Marketing, 57 (1), 1993, 1–22.

K. L. Keller, *Strategic Brand Management: Building, Measuring, and Managing Brand Equity,* (Upper Saddle River, NJ: Prentice Hall, 1997).

K. L. Keller, *Marketing Management,* 13th edn (Upper Saddle River, NJ, Prentice-Hall 2009).

K. L. Keller and D. R. Lehmann, "How, Brands Create Value?" *Marketing Management,* (May/June 2003) p. 23.

R. J. Kent, and C. T. Allen, "Competitive Interference Effects in Consumer Memory for Advertising: The Role of Brand Familiarity," *Journal of Marketing,* 58 (3), 1994, 97–105.

J. Knowles, "Value-based Brand Measurement and Management," *Interactive Marketing,* 5 (1), 2003, 40–50.

T. Koller, M. Goedhart and D. Wessels, *Valuation: Measuring and Managing the Value of Companies* 4th edn (New York: John Wiley & Sons, 2005).

P. Kottler, *A Framework for Marketing Management* (Upper Saddle River, NJ: Prentice-Hall, 2001) p. 188.

P. Kottler, and W. Pförtsch, *B2B Brand Management* (Berlin: Springer, 2006).

KPMG, "Purchase Price Allocation in International Accounting," 2007, available at: http://www.kpmg.ch/docs/Purchase_price_allocation_-_englisch_NEU.pdf.

H. Lambert, "Britons on the Prowl," *The New York Times,* November 29, 1987.

P. Little, D. Coffee and R. Lirely "Brand Value and the Representational Faithfulness of Balance Sheets," *Academy of Accounting and Financial Studies Journal,* September 2005.

E. F. Loftus and G. R. Loftus, "On the Permanence of Stored Information in the Human Brain," *American Psychologist,* 35, 5, 409–20, 1980.

Lord Hanson, Timesonline, November 2, 2004.

"Lord of the Raiders," *The Economist,* November 4, 2004.

T. Madden, F. Fehle and S. Fournier, "Brands Matter: An Empirical Investigation of Brand-building Activities and the Creation of Shareholder Value," *Journal of the Academy of Marketing Science,* 34 (2), 2006, 224–35.

Markenbewertung – Die Tank AG, Absatzwirtschaft, 2004.

T. McAuley, "Brand Family Values," *CFO Europe Magazine*, December 31, 2003.

McKinsey "Unlock Your Financial Brand," *Marketing Practice*, 2003, available at: McKinsey.com.

McKinsey "Do Fundamentals Really Drive the Stock Market?," 2004, available at: McKinsey.com.

C. F. Mela, S. Gupta and D. R. Lehmann, "The Long-Term Impact of Advertising and Promotions on Consumer Brand Choice," *Journal of Marketing Research*, 34, 1997, 248–61.

Milward Brown, Optimor, Top 100 most powerful brands 2008, available at: www.millwardbrown.com.

K. Moore, and S. Reid *The Birth of Brand: 4000 Years of Branding History* (McGill University, MPRA: Munich 2008) pp. 24–5.

S. Moorthy and H. Zhao "Advertising Spending and Perceived Quality," *Marketing Letters* 11(3), 2000, 221–33.

Morgan Stanley, "The Relationship of Corporate Brand Strategy and Stock Price," *U.S Investment Research*, June 13, 1995.

"Mother and Child Reunion: Will the AT&T/SBC Merger Build or Destroy Value?" *Knowledge@Wharton*, March 30, 2005.

J. Murphy (ed.), *Brand Valuation* (London: Hutchinson Business Books, 1989).

D. Muir, retrieved on September 16, 2009, p. 2 from: http://www.wpp.com/NR/rdonlyres/F157F2FF-BF45-409C-9737-C3550BAB15F3/0/TheStore_newsletter_006_ThePowerofBrands.pdf.

P. A. Naik, K. Raman and R. S. Winer, "Planning Marketing-Mix Strategies in the Presence of Interaction Effects," *Marketing Science*, 24 (1), 2005, 25–34.

Nielson Company, The Winning Brands, retrieved from www.nielson.com. nexcen.com.

Dr. M. A. Noll, "The AT&T Brand: Any Real Value?" *telecommunicationsonline*, November 1, 2005.

S. Northcutt, *Trademark and Brand* (SANS Technology Institute, 2007).

OECD.org.

Pernod Ricard, Press Release, March 31, 2008.

N. Penrose, *Valuation of Trademarks, in Brand Valuation* (London: Hutchinson Business Books, 1989) pp. 37–9.

R. Perrier, (ed.) *Brand Valuation* (London: Premier Books 1997).

M. E. Porter, *Competitive Advantage* (New York: Free Press, 1985).

C. Portocarrero, "Seeking Alpha," *WeSeed*, February 3, 2009.

PricewaterhouseCoopers, "Markenwert wird zunehmend als Unternehmenswert anerkannt," April 7, 2006.

PricewaterhouseCoopers "Advertising Pay Back," 2008.

PricewaterhouseCoopers, "Kaufpreisallokation: Mehr als nur Accounting," 2008.

J. A. Quelch, and K. E. Jocz, "Keeping a Keen Eye on Consumer Behaviour," February 5, 2009.

J. Quelch and A. Harrington, "Samsung Electronics Company: Global Marketing Operations," Harvard Business School, February 17, 2005.

V. R. Rao, M. K. Agarwal and D. Dahlhoff, "How Is Manifest Branding Strategy Related to the Intangible Value of a Corporation?" *Journal of Marketing*, 68 (4), 2004, 126–41.

E. S. Raymond, *The Jargon File*, December 29, 2003, see: www.catb.org/jargon/.

F. F. Reichheld, "The One Number You Need to Grow," *Harvard Business Review*, e-book, March 3, 2003.

Reuters.com

M. Ritson, "Mark Ritson on Branding: BrandZ Top 100 Global Brands Shows Strength in Numbers," *Marketing Magazine* April 28, 2009, available at: www.marketingmagazine.co.uk, royaltysource.com.

G. Salinas, *The International Brand Valuation Manual*, John Wiley & Sons, 2009.

Samsung Concludes Contract with the International Olympic Committee to Sponsor Olympic Games Through 2016, 23 April 2007, available at: Samsung.com.

S. Schwarzkopf "Turning Trade Marks into Brands: how Advertising Agencies, Created Brands in the Global Market Place, 1900–1930," CGR Working Paper 18.

D. Shenk, *Data Smog: Surviving the Information Glut* (New York: HarperCollins, 1998).

S. Srinivasan and D. M. Hanssens, "Marketing and Firm Value, Metrics, Methods, Findings, and Future Directions," *Journal of Marketing Research*, 46 (3), 2009.

R. E. Smith, "Integrating Information From Advertising and Trial: Processes and Effects on Consumer Response to Product Information," *Journal of Marketing Research*, 30, (2), 1993, 204–19.

Sports Business Daily, September 26, 2006.

"Study Shows Brand-building Pays Off For Stockholders," *Advertising Age*, 65, 1994, 18, superbrands.net.

"Top 100 Global Licensors", Licensemag.com. April, 2009.

D. S. Tull, Van R. Wood, D. Duhan, T. Gillpatrick, K. R. Robertson and J. G. Helgeson "Leveraged Decision Making in Advertising: The Flat Maximum Principle and its Implications," *Journal of Marketing Research* 23, 1986, 25–32.

D. Vakratsas and T. Ambler, "How Advertising Works, What Do We Really Know?" *Journal of Marketing*, 63 (1), January, 1999, 26–43.

L. Vaughan-Adams, "ICL name to vanish from tech heritage as Fujitsu rebrands," *The Independent*, June 22, 2001.

D. Walker, "Building Brand Equity through Advertising," IPSOS-ASI Research Article 5, 2002.

F. Wang, X.-P. Zhang and M. Ouyang, "Does Advertising Create Sustained Firm Value? The Capitalization of Brand Intangible," *Academy of Marketing Science*, September 21, 2007.

Which, "Switching from Bottled to Tap Water, Tap vs Bottled Water," available at: www.which.co.uk.

Woman's Wear Daily, "Hermès' Smart Car... Uniqlo's Warm Up... McQ Prints It Out," November 10, 2008.

The World Customs Organization and Organisation for Economic Co-operation and Development.

T. Yeshin, *Advertising*, (London: Thompson Learning, 2006).

A. Zednik and A. Strebinger, "Brand Management Models of Major Consulting firms, Advertising Agencies and Market Research Companies: A Categorisation and Positioning Analysis of Models Offered in Germany, Switzerland and Austria," *Brand Management*, 15 (5), 2008, 301–11.

INDEX